JUST DANCE

REAL LIFE STORIES OF THE LIFE GOD MAKES POSSIBLE WHEN WE RESPOND TO HIS VOICE

CALEB BYERLY

© 2023 Caleb Byerly

All rights reserved. No part of this publication may be reproduced, stored in a retrieval system, or transmitted in any form or by any means—for example, electronic, photocopy, recording—without the prior written permission of the publisher. The only exception is brief quotations in printed reviews.

ISBN 978-0-9981508-1-9 (paperback); 978-0-9981508-2-6 (ebook)

All Scripture quotations are from the ESV® Bible (The Holy Bible, English Standard Version®), copyright © 2001 by Crossway, a publishing ministry of Good News Publishers. Used by permission. All rights reserved.

CONTENTS

Acknowledgments	v
Introduction	ix
1. Upbringing	1
2. Israel	9
3. Preparation	17
4. Kiribati Bound	23
5. The Immersion	35
6. The Philippines	45
7. Obedience	53
8. Redeeming the Ancient Sounds	65
9. A Boy Named Juvy	79
10. Obja Transformation	87
11. Kiribati Blessing	99
12. Gladys	113
13. The Wait	119
14. Battles	131
15. Moving Forward	141
16. Be Evergreen	151
Partnering with Evergreen Missions	157
About the Author	159

ACKNOWLEDGMENTS

I want to thank my wonderful parents for recognizing the calling on my life and helping me steward it when I was young. You dealt with my immaturity like it was nothing, although I'm sure it was horrendous at times. You never acted afraid when I was called to the far-flung places of the world, and you always supported and walked with me through the thick and thin.

My sweetheart, I will never forget the day you said, "Where you go, I will go." I don't think we knew exactly what that meant or what it would look like. But your unwavering support, patient endurance, and tranquil voice has surely brought gladness to my heart.

My parents-in-love, you are the best parents-in-love anyone could ever have. From the first time we spent time together I knew there was a special connection between us, though I had no idea that I would one day marry your daughter. Now we are family, and you have always seen the best in us and have continually assisted us in bringing that forth.

Rodney and Marcia, thank you for being so intentional to raise us up with a kingdom heart. Your example as pastors has always shaped and molded me into being Christlike and carrying a love for the nations. Thank you for instilling the desire to always seek His presence wherever I am.

Ansulao, I couldn't ask for a better ministry partner to the unreached tribal places. You know the culture and language of the people, you translated for me, you protected me and our team members, you have gone before us to make sure everything was safe, and the list goes on. You are truly a *sulod*, a brother, and I will always value your friendship.

Palu and Ten, thank you for hosting us over and over again. You didn't just host us; you adopted us into your tribe. Thank you for taking care of my family and being true covenant friends!

I dedicate this book to the Father's heart for the unreached, brokenhearted, needy, and lost. This book is His story—a story of His heart for His people.

INTRODUCTION

This book was not easy to write. There were many days when I felt like giving up. The biggest reason for this is that at the time of writing this book, I'm thirty-five years old, and the biggest lie I've had to face is that I'm too young to write an autobiography.

I nearly listened to that lie and threw this book out the window many times, saying, "It's not for now." Many people kept encouraging me to not quit, however, and I continually felt a divine impression from the Father saying, "You need to do this now," so I continued. Still, I dragged my feet unintentionally, mostly because our plates were always full and there was always something else to do.

I did this until a random man walked up to me one day and said, "May I ask you a question?"

I said, "Yeah, sure. What is it?"

Looking at me with intent concern on his face, he asked, "What's your favorite color?"

Unsure of what to say because I like so many different colors, I randomly blurted out, "Blue."

The man tilted his head as though he thought that was interesting, and he casually pulled out a stunning, hand-made

INTRODUCTION

blue pen from his pocket. Handing it to me as a gift, he looked me in the eye and asked, "Have you finished writing your book yet?"

This man didn't know anything about me, so how did he know that I was writing a book? I responded softly, "Well, I'm nearly finished with it."

He replied, "Well, you need to finish it, and it has something to do with blue."

In the few months preceding that event, three other random individuals had also come to me and asked the exact same question, "Have you finished your book?" If that wasn't a clear word from the Lord, I don't know what would be. I knew the color blue represented the islands of the Pacific, because that's where almost all the stories that God has given me have come from.

All this told me—rather compellingly—that I needed to write this book even if I did think I was too young to write an autobiography, but what really exposed this thought as a lie was realizing that this is not really my story. Yes, I definitely talk a lot about me in this book because it's coming from me, but there's much more to this book than my story. This is the story of God's heart for the unreached peoples of the world, of the redemption of many tribes, of obedience, and of lost things being found. It's also a radical love story that you won't want to miss.

Through all of that, this is a story of an ordinary man. I spent many days writing this book with a baby in one arm and other babies crawling at my feet. Many days I had my notepad out while herding our animals on the Evergreen Missions Farm, jotting down ideas. I live a real life with real responsibilities just like you do.

Because this is the story of an ordinary man, it can also be your story. My prayer is that you are inspired as you read about how God has worked in and through my life, and more than

INTRODUCTION

being inspired, I pray that you are moved to seek God for your own stories.

As much as I could easily drum up these God stories into a dreamy missionary fantasy, I tried to keep this book as real and authentic as it was to live the stories that fill these pages. We searched thoroughly through my hundreds of journal entries and interviewed chiefs and missionaries to properly record testimonies from other perspectives. I didn't want to just show you the happy, easy side of walking with God. I wanted to reveal the reality of having a relationship with the Creator and fulfilling the Great Commission. Sure, it's thrilling and fun, but there are real hardships to carrying the cross daily.

As you read the stories in this book, you'll hear of some people groups that not many people know of. You'll see that there are still unreached people groups in the world who haven't heard the good news of the gospel of Jesus Christ.

In Revelation 7, John carves out the vision of seeing every nation—all tribes, peoples, and languages—standing before the throne and the Lamb of God, worshiping, and saying, "Salvation belongs to our God who sits on the throne, and to the Lamb!" (v. 10). Every time I read this verse, I'm reminded how the gospel has spread from Jerusalem to all the nations of the world, but that it has not reached all tribes, peoples, and languages yet. The prophecy of John in Revelation is a promise that *all* nations, *all* tribes, *all* peoples, and *all* languages will bow one day in worship to Jesus Christ. But I believe it also places the responsibility on us since Christ has commissioned us to go into all the world. There's still work to be done. When I read this verse, it stirs up a passion in me to participate with the Holy Spirit in bringing His Good News to all tribes.

For that reason, before you proceed in digesting the stories in the following pages, please promise me one thing. As you read this book, be encouraged, and even provoked, to see the Holy Spirit move in your life as well.

INTRODUCTION

Going to the far-flung islands and jungles is not for everyone. Reaching the unreached is not for everyone. Being a missionary in foreign lands is not for everyone. But there is one thing that is for everyone: the opportunity to hear God's voice. His voice will bring everything into alignment. It will bring your mind into the perfect realization that He truly loves you.

Maybe God's voice to you is like someone calling in the desert, "Prepare ye the way of the Lord." Or maybe His voice is through a dream. Perhaps His voice rings loud and clear every time you read that certain Bible verse. Or maybe you're brought to a deep sense of compassion when you hear about that certain nation. Whatever it is that He is saying, it's important to lean into it. Perhaps it's God speaking. Don't just hear Him and say, "Wow, God. Thank you for that," and then move on with life like nothing happened. Respond! Be alert and excited because He is moving and active.

In other words, hearing and responding to God is a dance between you and Him. Jesus, our beloved husband, invites you to dance with Him. Yes, it may take some time to learn the steps and, let me tell you something, He likes to change it up at times! You'll lean back and then lean forward, and out of the blue, He'll spin you, then chuckle and say, "Did you like that?" Other times it will be intimate and somber. The steps pulse at the cadence of His heart, so the only way to do it right is to know Him well. You'll never learn it by only reading, so get up and embrace Him. Just dance.

Okay, with all of that said, let me tell you some stories. Let's start with my childhood so you can get a good understanding of how all of this started.

ONE
UPBRINGING

My mother gave her life to Jesus shortly after giving birth to my older sister. She developed strong friendships with other women who were passionate for Jesus. They started a prayer group, gathering together every chance they could. One of her friends introduced my mom to the power of worship and, before too long, worship music continually filled our small trailer that sat on my great-grandfather's homestead. That is where I was privileged to live—on a homestead with four generations living together in the small town of Sophia, North Carolina.

Both my parents were lovers of Jesus, and I grew up with my siblings in a very good Christian home. I was the third of five children, sandwiched in the middle. We grew up learning about Jesus and going to an evangelical Christian church every Sunday. As a child, I was immersed in the Christian atmosphere. Nearly all my friends were from Christian homes. I thought that the whole world was like me. It wasn't until I became a teenager, however, that my relationship with Jesus became real to me.

Music was a big part of my family. All my brothers were

musicians, and we would get together to jam all the time. My one brother was a guitar player, my other brother was the bass player, my cousin was the second guitar player, and I was the drummer. We played blues and jazz music. Playing music was my outlet. I practiced all the time.

When I was thirteen, my friends from church and I started playing music together. We formed a band and started learning praise and worship songs like "My Redeemer Lives," Great Big God," and, "Here I Am to Worship." We were serious about our band and focused hard to learn new songs.

Not long after that, we approached the children's pastor of our church and told him that we wanted to lead worship for the children's church. He chuckled awkwardly at us, feeling a bit intimidated since he was not a musician or worship leader. But thankfully, because of his leadership skills, he recognized the importance of empowering us. He set up a healthy atmosphere for us to learn and grow in our gifts as worship leaders. We would set up our instruments every Sunday at 8:00 a.m., lead worship for our children's ministry, then break it down after the service. We did this week after week for years.

Before long, we were leading worship on Sunday mornings at the main church service under the oversight of our church's worship leaders. This led to leading worship at other churches throughout North and South Carolina. We would spend the weekend with different churches to minister to the children. Even though we were in ministry mode, we were also being ministered to by the Lord. Being activated in my spiritual gifting as a young teenager encouraged me to go deeper with the Lord. I began to develop my passion for Jesus at that time.

"PLAY AND PROPHESY"

My life made an altering shift when I was fifteen years old. My friends and I were about to minister at a children's camp. We were setting up all the band equipment and props for camp the night before the children arrived. We worked all day and were ready to rest. My friend Philip, who was the main singer of the band, suggested that we should worship before we went to bed. All of us were exhausted and ready to sleep, but we agreed that it would be good to sing some songs together. As we all began to sing, I felt a pulling in my heart to move. I just felt like I needed to dance. I didn't know why, it was just an inner feeling, so I started moving my legs and arms and dancing before the Lord.

Suddenly, something happened! The breath of God blew in the room like a strong wind, and we were filled with the Holy Spirit. We were filled with joy and started excitedly dancing all over the room. Visions appeared before us of what God was doing, and we saw angels ministering in that place.

With the compelling of the Lord, I sat down at the drum set and looked at it. The Holy Spirit said, "Play and prophesy," so I began playing the drums with all my heart. I could tell there was something different about my playing. I can't explain it other than that I was partnering with God to release His vibrations into the atmosphere. It shifted my paradigm. For the first time, after all those Sundays that I had played drums for worship teams and bands, I knew that my drumming was meant for something more than just setting a beat. I was partnering with the Spirit of God to release heaven's rhythms and cadence. Something shifted in my own heart at that moment, and I knew that the Lord was setting me apart as a priestly musician for His new sounds to be released into the world. I would no longer play for man, but only for God and His purposes.

Our worship went on for hours and hours through the night. A real stirring for His Spirit was in me and it never left me. I knew this was the start of being a vessel for the Holy Spirit to show His glory in the world. I didn't know what it would look like, but I was excited because I had a different heart and a new energy that I didn't have before.

Many months after that encounter, as I sat in my car and worshiped the Lord, I began to hear His voice whisper to me for the first time. It was not an audible voice, but I knew that it was His voice speaking to me. It was soft and gentle, like a father's. He began to tell me about His love for me and His people around the world. He began to show me pictures of my future. I went into a vision where I was older, and I was sitting down on the ground. I looked around and I saw bamboo huts and children running to me and they brought me a drum. I took the drum, began to play it, and crowds gathered around to worship. The vision stopped, and I felt an overwhelming sense of the Father's presence with me as I heard these words, "Caleb, you will go to the nations, and you will use drums to open the door of the gospel to my people."

At the same time, there was definitely a lot of youthful drama and plenty of misfits among the young people I hung out with. When we formed our worship band, all the musicians and singers fought over who would be in charge. We thought that it required a title, like "worship leader," and if you had that title then you would be the ultimate leader and everyone would listen to you. We fought for days until our leaders gently stepped into the feud and corrected us. It was definitely a struggle, but looking back now, I'm thankful that I had a community I could grow up in that nurtured us and didn't shun us.

The church leadership recognized the calling on my life and helped me grow in my relationship with God. At the time, I thought that meant that I would be ministering in that church for the rest of my life. I felt a real close connection to the church and the direction the church was going, and that's where I felt most comfortable. I felt like I had it all when it came to my church: a Spirit-filled community, worship, discipleship, and ministry training. What else could I ask for?

THE OTHER PART OF REAL LIFE

Sometimes people share these parts of their stories that are real God moments, and it can feel unrealistic to us. Maybe it feels like something someone like us could never experience. That's why I want you to know more of my life than just the flashy stories.

My father was a furniture maker and had his own business. My siblings and I were homeschooled, and being homeschooled, a large part of our learning was in the shop with dad. Though he had a billion things on his plate, he would always take time for us children to learn woodworking, upholstery, and other furniture skills. My siblings and I would work for him to make a little extra cash, then run to the store and buy soft drinks and candy bars.

I couldn't seem to connect with school, though. I started out in traditional schools but had a very difficult time adapting to classroom-style education. My mind just didn't fit in with the format of sitting and listening or the emotional pressure of competing with classmates. I resisted schooling so much that my parents eventually pulled me out and attempted to teach me from home. Even still, I resisted it. My mother patiently worked with me through the years of elementary, middle, and high school education as I barely held on. I graduated high school having fulfilled only the bare minimum requirements, and it felt like I was out of prison.

To me, graduation meant that it was finally time to really learn something. I learned by doing. I learned by making mistakes. In fact, after graduating high school, I developed a love of learning by listening to mentors, researching on the internet, and even reading books. I got a low-paying, backbreaking job installing tile and hardwood floors. As difficult as it was, I'm thankful that it helped me learn new skills. My boss helped me learn a skillset, plus I learned how to communicate with real people.

THE FOUNTAIN OF TEARS

At age twenty, after graduating from a year-long internship at my local church, I felt like I was on the path of becoming a full-time worship leader or youth pastor for my church. It was as if I didn't have any other options in life. I was going in this one direction, and I knew that ministry at my home church was the best option for me.

That was until a friend of the church, a man named Rick Wienecke, came to speak at the church. Rick was an artist who lived in Israel and focused a lot of his attention on the redemption of Israel. When he spoke at the church, there was a deep stirring in my heart to know more about Israel—the people, the land, the history, and the future of them all. I had learned about Israel by reading the Old Testament, but I didn't know anything about current-day Israel.

I connected with Rick that week when he was in town and got to know him. I asked him lots of questions about Israel like, "What's Israel like? Does God still have a promise for Israel? And how am I a part of Israel's promise?" Those were just a few of my questions that turned into a long, deep conversation and compelled me to dig deeper. While I was in the middle of all of that, I didn't realize that God was preparing me for a wild ride —to go and live in Israel! A few weeks later, Rick invited me to come to Israel, live with his family, and help him with one of his art projects called the Fountain of Tears.

The Fountain of Tears is a bronze sculpture garden that reflects the communication of suffering between Jesus's crucifixion and the Holocaust victims. I was honored to receive the invitation, but I had no clue what to expect from a trip to Israel. I did not learn much about Israel growing up, so I knew that it would be totally new to me. Also, living in a foreign country by myself would be new to me. I did not know how to process this invitation. Should I go, or should I continue to focus on my music and ministry in the church? I knew that I needed the Lord to guide and call me there, so I asked Him if He was calling me to go to Israel.

After a few weeks of praying and waiting, I never heard a direct yes or no from God, but I felt a real peace in my heart and knew that if I went, something great was waiting for me in that land. Even though I was afraid of leaving my comfort zone, the peace of God overcame my fear and gave me strength to go. I had never even considered leaving North Carolina before this point, let alone traveling across the world to the Middle East. I knew that this was going to be a life-changing season for me.

As I began to prepare for the trip, I told my family and friends that I was leaving. They were truthfully shocked that I would do that. I had so many great things in store for me with my work, ministry, and career. I kept asking myself, *Why am I leaving?* But I knew inside that God was calling me to Israel for a bigger reason than what I understood at the time.

Was I ready for this? Would the separation from my home and the shaking of my time in Israel destroy me? I left for Israel with questions like these, unable to foresee all the remarkable things that would unfold just a few short months later, launching me into a life that no one but God could make up.

TWO
ISRAEL

My twenty-first birthday was a great birthday for me, but a difficult one as well. On one hand, I knew that the next morning I would be leaving for a life-changing trip. Being an adventurous person, I was excited to leave the country. On the other hand, however, being a family person, my heart felt like it was ripping in two. I was torn. Truthfully, I wanted to stay home, but I knew that there was something more for me in Israel.

All my friends and family came over to my house the night of my birthday. We all celebrated, but we all felt a little sad as well. We sat around my parents' kitchen table, reminiscing over stories about all the fun we had through our teenage years. I didn't want to let go of what I had but I knew I had to. No one understood why I was leaving, but most of them trusted God would lead me.

The next morning, I got my bags ready and left for the airport. Everything seemed big to me, traveling through New York City and Frankfurt, Germany. On one flight, I was squeezed between two elderly Russian Jews with pink hair, one on each side of me. They both ended up falling asleep on my shoulders while I sat there awkwardly for eight hours.

Starting my first day in Israel, I immediately began working on the Fountain of Tears. Working on this project was pleasantly challenging for me. It was both a joy and an agonizing process to work on such a memorable, thought-provoking, and spiritually awakening project. My work involved grinding and polishing the bronze sculptures. I also helped create the fountain part, where the water flows down the Jerusalem stone wall where the depiction of Christ Jesus's crucifixion is embedded.

I worked with Rick four days a week, then backpacked throughout Israel on my days off. The land, the people, and the culture were all new to me. Somehow, despite my lack of money, I managed to make it to all the major spots in Israel, like the Sea of Galilee where Jesus started His ministry, Jerusalem with all its rich history, and Tel Aviv, which is the modern capital. Every time I wasn't working, I was backpacking. I slept on the ground at night while hiking through the arid Negev desert. I journeyed all over and met many people from different backgrounds.

The most fascinating observation to me was the people I met. This was an awakening for me and an abrupt way of destroying my comfortable Christian worldview where I only knew people who were like me. It introduced a worldview based on God's unconditional love covenant with the nation of Israel and the reality of how much people need Jesus.

CALLED TO THE ISLANDS

As I was working one day, I was grinding some bronze and doing my normal process of finishing the sculpture pieces when all of the sudden I felt the presence of the Holy Spirit begin to come over me as I was working. I was unable to continue to work because of the manifest presence of God in the shop with me. I had to stop my work and go back into my room. I stepped into the house, and I could still feel the Lord's presence on me like a river rushing through my veins.

I heard the Lord's voice speak to me. God spoke clearly to me, not as an audible voice but directly to my spirit. He said, "Caleb, you are going to go to islands in the middle of the Pacific Ocean."

I didn't know what that meant or how to respond to that. In all my years, I'd never thought much of the Pacific Islands. I wasn't even sure that there were islands in the Pacific besides Hawaii, so I walked over to the bookshelf and grabbed a map of the world. I opened it up and my eyes fell to the Pacific region of the map. Suddenly, as if the little dots on the map could move, some of the islands jumped out at my heart. I squinted and looked at the words above the islands and it read "Kiribati." I was not sure what Kiribati even was; I had never heard of it before.

I knew God was saying to me, "These are the islands." I could feel it deep in my spirit man—the pull, the call. I knew I had to respond, but I didn't know how or why.

Every day after my work, I would do hours of research about Kiribati. At that time, the internet was very limited in information about this island nation, but I learned as much as I possibly could from afar. As I read about the people and the culture, a deep love for these people filled me. I began to fall in love with Kiribati people, and I barely knew anything about the country. I wasn't sure if God was calling me to go there or calling me to pray for the people, but I was reminded over and over again why I heard about Kiribati in the first place. The only reason I looked at the map is because God said, "You are going to go to islands in the middle of the Pacific Ocean."

Two weeks passed after I received the word about Kiribati. I was working in the shop again when the Lord came over me the same way. I was filled with the manifest presence of God and was unable to work again. I put my tools down and went back into the house. The Lord spoke to me again, just as He did before. He said, "Caleb, I want you to begin to get connected with indigenous people."

Indigenous people? I did not know exactly what that meant. I knew it was both an invitation and a command from the Lord. From that day on, I felt a great burden and desire to know more about the indigenous people of the world. I could hear over and over again, *Tribes, tribes, tribes.* I began to have dreams of them every night, dreams of tribes coming to know Jesus, and lost, ancient doors being open that no man could open. I just did not know what that meant or how that applied to me. I wanted to know more, so I tried researching. I read books and searched the internet for more clues about where God was leading me, but I wasn't getting anywhere. I felt lost and like this was a huge agenda that I could not carry on my own.

WORLD CHRISTIAN GATHERING OF INDIGENOUS PEOPLE

Not long after that, I learned that there was a special gathering being held in Israel that year called the World Christian Gathering of Indigenous People (WCGIP). How odd and amazing that the Lord spoke to me about indigenous people and there just happened to be a gathering of indigenous people in Israel that year!

I thought that I wouldn't be able to attend the gathering because I wasn't an indigenous person. I am an American with lots of different mixed blood in me. Why would I be allowed to attend this gathering? I moved ahead, however, and contacted the chairman of the gathering. Amazingly, he allowed me to come. I was thrilled! I thought that I could at least go and hide myself in the back corner just to see what God would do.

The WCGIP started in Tel Aviv near one of the water ports.

When I arrived, I saw a bunch of people with feathers, arrows, tattoos, and painted faces. These were tribal delegates from different nations. Some were chiefs and some were elders from different tribes from all around the world. It was a wild and glorious moment of seeing people from all nations together at the main port of Israel. There was even a canoe of Pacific Islanders that sailed a portion of the Mediterranean Sea and arrived at the port of Tel Aviv.

We all got on buses and traveled around Israel for ten days. One day, we were all at the Sea of Galilee, where Jesus did most of His ministry. We all got on boats and went out into the sea, just like Jesus and His disciples did. We were from different nations, tribes, and languages, but we squeezed onto three boats and took them out to the middle of the sea.

We roped the boats to each other and began to sing hymns together. As we worshiped, there happened to be some people who had their native drums with them. I remember seeing an African, a Japanese, an Indonesian, a Native American, and a Norwegian person with their drums, and they all came together. To hear these drums from different nations combined was fascinating to me. But then as they began to sync together and make a corporate sound of worship, something resonated in me that shook my inner core.

As we all worshiped, some of the dancers jumped in the middle of the drum circle and started dancing. I first saw a Filipino dancer, then an African, then a Scandinavian, then an Aboriginal Australian—one nation after another, dancing their dance before the Lord, right there on the Sea of Galilee where Jesus's ministry was birthed. I was filled with joy to think of the fact that the ministry of Jesus went from Jerusalem to Judea, to Samaria, then to all the parts of the world, and now the nations returned to Israel to worship and adore the one true God who saved their people groups.

ISRAEL

"But you will receive power when the Holy Spirit has come upon you, and you will be my witnesses in Jerusalem and in all Judea and Samaria, and to the end of the earth." (Acts 1:8)

As amazing as this was, I realized quickly that this couldn't be the end. There was more. There were more souls to save. There were more nations to redeem. There were more tribes to reach! During those short ten days of being with tribal chiefs from nations around the world, I quickly learned from them that there's more work to be done. Our commission is not yet finished.

And Jesus came and said to them, "All authority in heaven and on earth has been given to me. Go therefore and make disciples of all nations, baptizing them in the name of the Father and of the Son and of the Holy Spirit, teaching them to observe all that I have commanded you. And behold, I am with you always, to the end of the age." (Matthew 28:18–20)

Barnabas, a leader and father of the Pacific Islands approached me. This man was one of the leaders of the WCGIP, as well as a highly respected leader in the Pacific Islands. He sat me down at a table and took a lot of time imparting wisdom to me. I soaked it in like a sponge. I shared with him the word that I received from the Lord about the Kiribati islands in the Pacific. Perhaps Barnabas took so much time for me because he recognized that the Lord was taking me to the Pacific; he even blessed me and imparted a father's blessing for the Pacific. He shared the heart and struggles of the islands of the Pacific and told me how important it is for the islands to receive the gospel and the love of Jesus. He sealed up all of what he told me by looking in my eyes saying, "My son, you are the next generation. Take it and run with it."

MEETING PALU

Our time at the Sea of Galilee was glorious. It was so glorious, in fact, that I needed to process everything that happened there. I decided to search for a place where I could pray by myself. I walked down to the coast, sinking my feet in the sand.

As I stood there, I looked into the distance of the Galilee, thinking about Jesus's ministry, thinking about His heart for the nations and trying to get a grasp of everything that was unfolding before me. Suddenly, I could hear footsteps walking behind me. Disrupted from my thoughts, I turned to see who it was and found it was a young man about the same age as me. He came up to me, stood beside me, and sank his toes into the sand just as I had. I asked what his name was, and he said in broken English that his name was Palu.

I could tell that he really wanted to get to know me, and I wanted to get to know him too. He and I shared about our lives. I learned that he was one of the delegates from a tribe in the Philippines called the Manobo. He began to tell me what his life was like in a tribe far in the mountains of Southeast Asia, and I told him what my life was like as a country boy from North Carolina. Even though we were having a hard time communicating, we somehow became very good friends almost instantly.

Palu and I stuck together for the rest of the week. He had a newly wedded wife named Ten. Both Palu and Ten were from tribal areas in the Philippines, but they were from different tribes. They were very special. We stuck together for the rest of the week, traveling from the Sea of Galilee to Jerusalem, and then to the Negev desert.

On the last day of the WCGIP, as everyone said their goodbyes, I dreaded saying goodbye to Palu and Ten. I felt a special connection with them—a kindred heart—and I could feel the Lord's pleasure on our friendship. I gave them a hug and started walking away to my transportation. After a few minutes, I looked back and Palu had tears in his eyes. He ran back to me, we hugged again, and I said, "If I ever travel to Asia, I will come visit you!" Then I got in a taxi and left.

Driving away from the WCGIP, I had many thoughts about the future, and about God's calling and what it was supposed to look like. I was excited but confused, stirred but not sure what to do. Was the WCGIP the fulfillment of the word the Lord gave me that day as I was working on the bronze sculpture? Was all of this just nonsense and I should simply go back home and get a real job?

At that point, seeing what I saw that week was much more than exciting; it imparted a deep craving to see the kingdom come to the indigenous people who haven't heard yet. My entire being felt that all I should do was respond to the word He gave me. I kept hearing that word ring over and over in my head, *Respond, respond, respond.*

Although I didn't know exactly how to respond, I knew I needed to keep moving forward, letting go of anything that held me back. All the while, I had no clue what was about to happen.

THREE
PREPARATION

After my glorious time in Israel and being a part of the WCGIP, I made my way back to the United States. Back in North Carolina, I knew I had some big decisions to make. My family gave me a warm welcome back home. I felt so comfortable being back after my many months living in the Negev desert. As I stepped through the front doors of my church, I felt like I had been gone for many years as I joyfully reunited with my friends and mentors.

I spent much time sharing stories of my adventures in Israel. Everyone wanted to know what Israel was like, and they especially wanted to know about the WCGIP. It was challenging for me to articulate to my family what I heard from the Lord because I was in the molding stage. The unveiling of God's heart for the indigenous people gripped me to the core, but I didn't know how to explain what I felt. I was learning the value of creating language for what God was developing in me. As much as my friends loved me being home, they also wanted me to join them in their projects, dreams, and future. Because I didn't know how to tell them what I experienced in Israel, they wanted me to pick up where I had left off, as though the life-changing things I'd experienced in Israel hadn't happened.

And, oh, opportunity! There was so much opportunity and so much potential in the air. As much as I wanted to do all the things available to me, the desire deep within me was to fulfill the word God spoke to me that kept ringing in my soul. I didn't know what that meant, but I knew I needed to obey. I couldn't get Kiribati off my mind. I thought about, prayed into, and researched as much as I possibly could.

One night as I sat in my room praying, I came to the realization, *I'm going to Kiribati*. I made up my mind and it was certain: *I'm going*. I knew that God didn't want me to just pray for the nation, He wanted me to go. But that would mean I had to leave my home again, that would mean I would be alone again.

GOING TWO BY TWO

Being by myself in Kiribati didn't seem like the right thing to do. I felt like I needed a partner. I was reminded of the verse, when Jesus gave authority to His disciples, that says, "After this the Lord appointed seventy-two others and sent them on ahead of him, two by two, into every town and place where he himself was about to go" (Luke 10:1).

At this point in my missionary journey, I had a greater understanding of the "two by two." I understood why Jesus designed it to be that way with new missionary work into unknown territory. It was because the two support each other. At the same time, they were light enough to not be overburdened by the overhead cost of a large team.

This meant that I needed one other person to go with me. I thought and prayed about it for a long time. I had many friends who were potential candidates for the journey. I felt like the person had to be just the right person, someone who was flexible and ready for quick changes and surprises, willing to go where we needed when we needed, someone who was just as sold out in love with Jesus as I was, someone who is filled with the Spirit and sensitive to His voice. Just then, I came to realize who that person was: my good friend Joel.

Joel was passionate for Jesus and was always ready for whatever God had in store. Before I went to Israel, we always evangelized together at coffee shops and restaurants. Joel was a very friendly person. He loved people and took things lightheartedly. The joy of the Lord was deeply evident in his life. I felt like he would be the perfect person to ask to go with me on this journey.

Joel knew that I had heard from the Lord about Kiribati. When I asked him to go with me, however, I believe he was especially surprised. He told me that he would ask the Lord about it, but I could hear it in his voice that his answer was already a yes. A week later we got together, and he gave me the answer. He jokingly walked into the room with a deep frown on his face. With a slow, monotone voice, he mumbled, "I hate to say this ... but you're going to have to deal with this goofball on your journey to the Kiribati islands."

His face lit up, and I exclaimed, "Yes!"

We got together every Thursday evening to have meetings on how to prepare for our trip to Kiribati. We had goals set to work and earn enough money for our plane tickets and two month's stay in Kiribati. We also discussed details about traveling and cultural learning. Unfortunately, we were not able to get a whole lot of information about how to travel to Kiribati. The internet at that time was very limited, and it was obvious that not many people had traveled to Kiribati because there weren't many books or resources available.

We attempted to find at least one person who had been to Kiribati or was from there. To our surprise, we could not find anyone. We tried locating a place to book a motel or hotel on the island, but we couldn't. After all the research that we did, we concluded that we would not be able to find anyone from the island or find a place to stay; we would just have to go and figure it all out when we got there.

    Something about that thrilled me. I knew I needed to be wise about it, but we had tried everything. At that point, if God was truly calling us there, we would just have to go and trust Him to take care of us.

GOD'S PROVISION TO GO

The money was the biggest obstacle we faced. How would two young, broke men be able to raise funds within a short time frame to travel across the world to one of the most far-flung islands on the planet? I knew I had to raise the money, but I did not know how. One of the major tests and verifications of God's calling rested under this truth: If God is calling me, He will provide for me.

    Joel and I committed that we would work our hardest, do our best, and let God do the rest. At that time, I started working again for a person who installed wood and tile flooring. I worked diligently every day and tried saving every dollar I got. Both Joel and I were focused on our plans. Thankfully I raised enough funds for my tickets and the expected food and lodging costs. Joel was still lacking some funds for his plane tickets, and we were getting close to our travel date, so we had to decide what we were going to do. I wondered, *Will I be traveling by myself?*

    Just as it seemed that we were out of options, Joel called me on the phone, excitement bursting in his voice. "I'm going to sell my Mustang," he said.

    "You're going to do what?"

    "Yes, I'm going to sell my convertible Mustang. I have prayed about it, and I feel like this is the quickest and easiest way to get the money we need to get."

I was floored by Joel's faith and persistence to give up the very thing that he enjoyed so much. Joel was the stud, and all the girls loved to ride around in his convertible Mustang. I'm sure he was deeply attached to that vehicle, and now he was going to give it up for this mission trip?

But he did! It sold quickly, and it gave him enough money to buy all the plane tickets that he needed for the trip plus extra funds for his expected lodging and food for the trip.

We were ready. It was game time. We purchased the tickets and started gearing up for our trip to the remote islands of the South Pacific. We would have loved to have the pure vision of the Lord and a great, strategic plan for our ministry to the Kiribati islands, but all we were hearing from God was, "Go." None of our family members or friends knew what we were doing, and neither did we. Would this be a disaster? Would we quickly become martyrs? Would we get lost at sea?

As Joel and I fought through fear and the struggle of getting everything together, neither of us knew just how profoundly Someone had already gone a few days ahead of us to prepare the way.

FOUR
KIRIBATI BOUND

It was 2:00 a.m. My alarm clock went off thirty minutes after I had finally gotten to sleep. Joel and I were up all the night before packing our bags. We didn't care; we were excited. It was finally the day we had been preparing for. We were going to Kiribati!

We quickly jumped in the car and went to the airport. Our journey started in our little airport in North Carolina, going across the country, then all the way across the Pacific to Sydney, Australia. After that, we transferred to another flight that went to the Fiji islands. At that point we were nearly three days into our journey, and we had not arrived in Kiribati yet. Before our last flight, we slept on the airport floor. We were exhausted.

Despite the agonizing travel, we were thrilled to approach the main island of Kiribati—the itsy-bitsy little island of Tarawa. Our last flight was a mercifully short one. We gazed out the window of the plane and could see the mesmerizing coral atoll protruding gracefully out of the big blue sea. The atoll was a strip of coral land that encircled a tropical blue lagoon. The island was full of little thatched-roofed huts and small buildings. I could see one road that went through the middle of the island with a few vehicles going back and forth. The outskirts of the island were full of the blue colors of the sea, starting from bright light blue and going to a deep, dark blue as the water got deeper.

The landing strip was one lane and frighteningly short. I wondered how the plane would even land on the small strip. We descended, and I could see pigs racing the plane on the landing strip as we approached. It was a rough landing, but we survived (and so did all the pigs). Getting out of the airplane, we were greeted with a heavy gust of hot, humid air. It was thick, like walking into a sauna. But we couldn't be happier. We were in Kiribati. We had made it!

The airport was a small shack, literally a concrete structure and a roof where everyone gathered to wait for the people to come out of the planes.

The Kiribati people looked amazing. They were what you would typically think of for Pacific Islanders—dark skin with a slightly Asian or Aboriginal look to their face. They were graceful in the way they walked and talked. The men looked very strong. The women seemed to be the busiest, taking care of the kids and talking to each other.

Most of the people coming off the planes were Kiribati seamen, foreign politicians, and Chinese businessmen. Then there was Joel and me—two random American lads, with no one to pick us up.

Everyone was greeted with hugs and handshakes as they got their luggage and filtered through the airport. Joel and I stood there by the street. All the cars left, and the airport quickly became quiet.

THE LORD GOES BEFORE US

I was immediately faced with great fear. This fear was something I had never felt before, a fear that paralyzed my thoughts.

I was overwhelmed with thoughts of doom; I couldn't think of anything else. *Why are we here? Where are we going? Where are we going to stay tonight?* Perhaps we would die of starvation or lack of good shelter in this country. We didn't even know anyone from this country, so there we were—standing, with no one to meet us.

We both looked at each other, our faces etched with fear. Just then, two people came up to us. One was a large Kiribati man, and the other was a bubbly young Kiribati woman, both with big smiles on their faces. Surprisingly, they spoke with excellent English. They asked us what our names were, and we hesitantly told them. Why were they asking us this? Were they going to kidnap us?

They stared at a piece of paper in their hand as they mumbled words to each other in the Kiribati language. They both shrugged their shoulders and said, "We were supposed to pick two people up from the airport, but they did not arrive. The description of the two people was just like you two, but they never got off the airplane. Since they never got off the airplane, would you like to stay in their place?"

Joel and I looked at each other with a little bit of skepticism. We were concerned it was a scam. We stepped to the side, prayed, and immediately felt the peace of the Lord on it. We felt Him say, "I prepared a place for you. Go with them."

They took us in their vehicle to a small inn where they worked. When we arrived, I thought, *Oh, this is definitely a scam. They brought us here so we would be forced into paying them for a place to stay.*

They took us up to the little room they had prepared. It was a compact room with a wooden bedframe without a mattress. There was no extra room to move around, but it had all of the essentials. It was a rough and dirty space, but exactly what we needed. They turned to us and said, "You do not need to pay us. You stay here as long as you need."

We were amazed, and thankful because we didn't have any money to give. The Lord truly prepared a place for us, and we fell into it like a trap without knowing how. It was exactly what we needed, just a simple place to lay our heads at night.

GETTING TO KNOW THE ISLAND

Tarawa island was full of people. This was one of the only islands in Kiribati that had electricity, and it was the main hub for ships passing through. All the education centers were on this island, as well as the main hospital, so it was where all the people living in the outer islands would come for education, medical help, and job opportunities. The one road that went through the island was busy with public transportation, vendors selling fish, cats and dogs running around, and children playing. For such a small island, it was busy.

After a few days of exploring the island and meeting some Kiribati people, Joel and I both felt the need to go somewhere to pray and seek the Lord's face. As adventuristic as it was just to be on the island, something burned in my heart to seek why we were there in the first place. We decided to go to the northern part of the island, called North Tarawa, where we heard there were much fewer people. We wanted to travel up there, camp out on the beach for a few days, and just wait on the Lord for direction. After asking around, we were able to find a small boat driver who offered to take us across the lagoon. We arranged to go the next day in the morning at 9:00 a.m.

That next morning, we quickly packed our bags and rushed over to the location where the boat was to depart. We arrived at 9:00 a.m. on the dot with all our camping equipment strapped to our backs. We found a twenty-five-foot boat floating on the edge of the coast, with the beautiful blue lagoon surrounding it as a backdrop. A great thrill filled our hearts as we got to the boat, but there was one problem—there was no driver.

"Let's wait for a few minutes for the driver to arrive," I said.

We waited ten minutes, but no driver came.

"Let's wait a little longer," I suggested. "Perhaps something came up and the driver is running late."

After thirty minutes, there was still no driver.

One hour later, no driver. Two hours later, no driver. We were discouraged. After all, we paid this guy to take us on a private boat across the lagoon and he didn't show up. We assumed he just left his boat there for us, but I didn't know how to drive a boat, and I would have been really afraid of Joel attempting to drive it.

At the third hour, a Kiribati family slowly walked up to the boat, staring at us as they came. They were afraid to look directly at us, and I could tell they were concerned about us foreigners being there. They minded their own business, though, chatting in the Kiribati language that we didn't understand. More and more people came, carrying lots of bags, mostly full of food and clothing. They all got into the boat one by one until the boat was completely full of Kiribati people. Joel and I stood to the side, confused and saddened by the thought that the people were taking our private boat that we rented.

Finally, the driver of the boat arrived beaming with a joyful and stressless smile. He said, "We go?" with his Kiribati accent. I nodded as I pointed confusedly at the boat, questioning if we were to get in. He nodded back with another big smile on his face. We struggled reluctantly to get ourselves onto the boat, attempting to find a spot to fit our bodies and belongings. The boat was meant for just a few people, not the thirty people who were crammed in there now. It floated sluggishly a few inches above the crest of the water.

As we boarded the boat, everyone stared at us. I'm sure they wondered where we were going. The atmosphere was a little tense with all the different factors involved.

Some people sat on the outer ledge of the boat, and some people stood up in the middle of the boat. As I sat, others stayed standing because there was not enough space to sit down. Despite being overcrowded, the boat departed for the northern part of the island.

A STORM AND A PEACE OFFERING

I could see North Tarawa in the far distance. It looked like it was close, but I could tell it would take a while to get there because of how slowly we needed to go due to the boat being overfilled. My nerves were shot, seeing the waves splash over the side of the boat. I was convinced that we were moments from disaster. Just when I thought it couldn't get worse, I looked up and saw something that I prayed wouldn't happen—a storm!

Apparently, storms form quickly in the Pacific. It was nice and sunny when we started, but it quickly shifted into a downpour of heavy tropical rain. Everyone quickly moved around on the boat. Kids scrambled to hide under their parents. Mothers were quickly grabbing their clothing to place over their heads. The men didn't seem to care; they just sat there with their muscular, tattooed bodies, looking into the distance.

Joel and I quickly grabbed for our bags as the rain showered on us. My trusty microfiber towel was waiting for me in there. A sense of relief came over me, thinking, *At least I'll be dry.* Just then, I looked across the boat and I saw a beautiful elderly woman. She sat on the edge of the boat, shivering, with nothing above her head. Compassion for her came over me. I didn't know what to do other than offer my towel to her, but I didn't know how to do it. I summoned enough courage in my timid self and looked at her.

As our eyes met, I motioned with my hands as I slowly said, "Here's a towel. You can put it above your head to protect you from the rain." After that I looked around the boat and noticed everyone intently staring at us like watching a movie. I handed the towel to her, and she hesitated to receive it. After a few seconds, she reluctantly reached her hands out.

There was an exchange. With a stern face, she took ahold of the towel. The stern face eased into a pleasant smile. Suddenly at that moment, there was a shift in the atmosphere. The little, rickety boat that floated on the open lagoon became a happy place for everyone. Smiles filled all the faces around us, and ours as well. It was as if the towel was a gift of peace, an exchange for the connection with the Kiribati people. As soon as that transaction happened, we were connected with them. There was a woman sitting beside the lady I gave the towel to who started talking to us in broken English.

"Thank you very much. My mom needed a towel."

"You're welcome," I said. "I thought she would need it."

"Where are you two going?"

"We are just traveling to see North Tarawa, but we're not sure where exactly."

"Oh, I see," she said. "Would you like to come with us to celebrate Independence Day for Kiribati? We want you to be our guest of honor."

Joel and I didn't even know that it was Independence Day for Kiribati, but Joel looked at the woman and said, "Of course! We would love that."

We didn't have anywhere else to go. It's not that we had some kind of important event or meeting to attend, and being the guests of honor sounded a whole lot better than scavenging around on an open beach.

OUR UNCOMFORTABLE OPPORTUNITY

We arrived at North Tarawa safely (thank God!). We all departed, and the woman who was speaking to us on the boat, whose name was Akita, directed us to a beautifully crafted hut for us to rest in while we waited for the big Independence Day celebration to start.

Joel and I were amazed as we watched the true Kiribati culture play out before our eyes. The whole village came together to help prepare. All ages participated in weaving mats, gathering flowers, and setting up the decorations. All the men went spear fishing and came back with clams, octopus, and an assortment of fish. It was spectacular to watch this untouched people group in their true culture coming alive before my eyes.

The Independence Day celebration started, and Akita came to our hut to show us the way to the stage where our seats of honor were located. She pointed, "Your seats, there. You sit beside the vice president of Kiribati and the ambassador of Taiwan." To our shocked surprise, there sat two men in elegant and dignified attire. I was so embarrassed, looking down at my raggedy clothes with holes in them. I thought, *We shouldn't be here!* Perhaps it was better for us to be scavenging the beaches. How could we sit beside these high, elite men of honor?

Despite feeling deeply embarrassed, we approached our seats of honor, postured ourselves in a dignified way, and kindly greeted our fellow guests of honor. The ambassador turned to us with a dignified and joyful grin and, quickly starting a conversation, he introduced himself with lots of cheer. It was a joy to meet another foreigner and to share about our journey with them. The vice president was also very kind, with lots of laughter and joy that boomed from his deep, Kiribati-accented voice. They didn't care about the holes in our pants. They didn't care that we didn't have clean-cut hair or appropriate clothing. They were just happy that we were there.

As my eyes scanned the island from the elevated platform, seeing the islanders bustle around in preparation, I realized something: the Holy Spirit had prepared this platform for His kingdom purposes, and He wanted us to have it for a special purpose. He took us from rags to royalty for a purpose, not just for our pleasure, but for His purpose. We embraced it and began to enjoy the opportunity to connect with the high-level men and women there.

The celebration started, and we got the opportunity to learn about the history of the beautiful nation of Kiribati and how they gained independence on July 12, 1979.

When the celebration ended, we all helped to pack up the many decorations and belongings, then made our way back to the boat. I didn't know what was next, but I knew it looked like our time at North Tarawa was done. We would, however, miss Akita's family deeply. They were so special, and we felt a deep connection with the whole family, even in this short time. We said our goodbyes, gave them hugs, and then walked away toward the boat. As we grabbed our bags with sadness on our faces, Akita's gentle voice spoke up some distance away.

"Please, come stay with us at our family's home. We would like for you to stay with us!"

At this point, there wasn't any debate on what we would do. We didn't have anywhere else to go, so of course we would go with them, as they already felt like family to us. The men received us as fellow men of the family. The women took care of our needs. The kids loved to play with us. There was a special connection with this family. Instead of getting on the boat that day, we traveled a different direction with our Kiribati family—we traveled back to their home village.

THE NEXT STEP IN OUR MISSION

I knew we were stepping into a new season of our missionary season—the immersion. We were still foreigners, but we decided to accept the call to become and behold the Kiribati culture. This is what the immersion is—getting fully saturated. We were fully dipped in the culture and life of Kiribati. Every second was excitement and thrill as we soaked it up like a sponge. Down deep, I knew the Lord was doing something. I didn't feel the Lord say, "Go," anymore. Now, I was hearing the Lord say, "Learn."

I knew that the months ahead of me would be all about learning: learning the Kiribati culture, learning the language, and even more importantly, learning the protocol of bringing His gospel to His people in Kiribati. I was reminded of this passage in the Bible where Paul shared a secret to his missionary protocol:

> To the Jews I became as a Jew, in order to win Jews. To those under the law I became as one under the law (though not being myself under the law) that I might win those under the law. To those outside the law I became as one outside the law (not being outside the law of God but under the law of Christ) that I might win those outside the law. To the weak I became weak, that I might win the weak. I have become all things to all people, that by all means I might save some. (1 Corinthians 9:20–22)

I knew I needed to become a Kiribati man in order to reach the Kiribati people. Although I knew I would—and should—never fully become one, I knew that rejecting the opportunity to learn the culture would display to them that I didn't care about them.

What I didn't know was how hard it would be. Could we

handle the learning curve of immersing in the Kiribati culture? Was it even worth it? Was this the right thing to do?

Many thoughts engulfed me as we slowly floated across the lagoon on a small Kiribati sail canoe. Unlike the boat we used to get across, this small canoe held only Joel, the few members of Akita's family, and me. As I gazed east at the horizon, thoughts of home overcame me. I missed home. I had to persevere through my emotions. Steering my eyes from the horizon to the canoe full of brown-skinned Micronesians, I boldly whispered a declaration in my heart and mind: "This is my family now."

FIVE
THE IMMERSION

Docking up at the main island, we came to a halt as the front of the sail canoe dug into the sand of the beach. We stepped out into the sun-warmed water of the island and tied the small canoe to a leaning coconut tree. We had arrived at a small village on the other side of Tarawa island. We made our way by foot to the neatly organized village that was nestled beside the coast. Akita's family greeted us warmly, with big smiles on their faces.

They hurriedly prepared a place for us to stay. Within just a few days, they built a small hut for us to live in, called a *kiakia*, which is a raised platform with a thatched roof that does not have walls. This allows the island breeze to flow through the hut and keep people cool on the hot days. It was very pleasant during the daytime, but it was very challenging at night. Many a night, we would have rats or cats jump on our heads.

The platform for the kiakia was made of strips of thinly split tree branches laid beside each other, making a hard and lumpy surface. This took time to get used to. My shoulders and hips were sore and bruised the first few weeks after sleeping on it night after night. We didn't have blow-up mattresses or sleeping bags; we just had the hard surface to lay on. I used my extra clothes as a pillow and a thin man-skirt as a blanket. After some time, we got used to it and started to really enjoy the hard bed.

Our toilet and shower area were just a hole in the ground located in a non-secluded area beside some of the huts. To say the least, this took a long time to get used to, and needless to say, we quickly became family with the locals through our many awkward moments. The Kiribati family treated us so kindly, and we made all the effort to help them in any way we could. We would attempt to cook food with them even though we didn't know their culinary style. Cooking octopus and squid is very different from cooking eggs and pre-packed noodles, which were the only things I knew how to cook. Despite my lack of proper education on the subject, we quickly learned new cultural skills every day.

We focused on learning their language. We started by learning simple greetings like *Mauri* (hello) and *Ko Uara?* (how are you?). This expanded into learning some phrases like *E mena ia Ioera?* (Where is Joel?). I used this phrase much, as Joel was often lost on the beaches, running around with the kids, or playing hide-and-seek. The kids loved him because he had such a playful, childlike spirit. Joel and I were a good balance of play and purpose. Obviously, he was the playful one, while I was the purpose-driven type. Like iron sharpens iron, we often sharpened each other with our differences.

The men in our family taught us how to *koro karewe* (cut the coconut sap). This tradition meant that the men climbed the coconut tree every morning and afternoon and lightly cut the sapling of the coconut pods to produce the sap from the tree. This was their way of getting the nutrients of the coconut and filtering the brackish water from the island. The water from the island was very salty and contaminated.

There was a shallow water well in the village that we lived

in. Multiple times a day, we would draw water from the well for drinking. But before we could drink it, we had to boil it for at least an hour to kill all the bad bacteria. This took a lot of time, so getting the natural sap from the coconut tree was very beneficial, since the tree itself is the natural filtering system. By the time the island water flows through the trees, it comes out of the top of the tree as a sweet, vitamin-packed sap that we would catch in recycled water bottles.

After some time, this skill called *koro karewe* became my job. I would climb coconut trees every morning with a sharp knife in my hand and lots of water bottles, lightly shaving the sapling pods with the knife and placing the bottles underneath it to catch the sap. Over the course of a few weeks, I got good at it and started to get full bottles of sap every day, which gave the whole family lots of good, nutritious drink.

STUMBLING UPON COMMUNITY

The Kiribati islanders were already Christian due to the many evangelistic excursions of the London Missionary Society and the Roman Catholic Church in the 1700s and 1800s. You could easily notice that there were church buildings scattered throughout the island. Christian beliefs were engrained in their cultural practices.

Mixed in with their Christian belief, however, was a lot of black magic and traditional beliefs. To add to that, every church service that we attended was extremely boring. The church members would attend the service and leave the service without truly receiving something from the Word of God or the presence of God. This was truly a sign that the spirit of religion had made its mark on this culture.

During this time, our Kiribati family invited us to a birthday party for an extended family member. The party was to be held at another village called Eita. Arriving at nighttime, we could see lots of people hustling around, preparing for the party to start. The party was filled with dancing, laughter, and Kiribati jokes. We set a smile on our faces, pretending to understand their humor. As the attendees would laugh, Joel and I would look at each other and pretend to laugh, which would make us genuinely laugh, so we felt like we were joining the party.

After some time, I decided to take a stroll around the area surrounding where the party was held. I wanted to explore since I had never been to that part of the island before. As the party proceeded, I excused myself and walked out of the main meeting area to get a breath of fresh air.

I stood outside with my arms crossed and a smile on my face, observing everyone and everything that was going on at the party. Just then, a short, muscular man walked over and stood beside me. He looked at me with a curious expression on his face and began to talk quietly to me with very good English. I was surprised and complimented him on it.

The man's name was Katuba. He thought Joel and I were Mormon missionaries, since we were two foreigners around the same age that most Mormon missionaries are. I explained to him that we weren't Mormon missionaries, but we were missionaries, with the desire to bring God's goodness to Kiribati. I told him that we weren't bringing religion, but Jesus. I explained the goodness of God and shared some of my personal testimonies. He nodded the whole time that I poured out the gospel to him in simple terms.

Katuba said, "Yes! Yes! I know the Jesus you are talking about. I am also a believer, and we have a church here in Eita, and I am the pastor!"

I'm positive that a look of excitement swept over my face. I was thrilled to finally meet a Kiribati man who was a pastor of a church. I had previously met other church leaders in Kiribati, but I could feel that they were simply wanting to smooth talk me, perhaps to manipulate me to get funding or fame because I was a foreigner. But Katuba didn't seem to be that way; I could see that he had a pure heart. He and I chatted for a long time as the party proceeded. When it came to an end, Katuba asked, "Can you and Joel come to our church on Sunday morning?"

I replied, "Yes, it would be an honor to join you in worship."

Sunday morning approached quickly, and Joel and I traveled by public transportation to Eita. We didn't know what to expect, since our previous experiences with church services in Kiribati were very boring. We prepared our clothing as best as we could, asking our Kiribati family for suggestions, and headed for church.

Arriving at the church, we were careful to observe the local practices, starting with seeing them take off their shoes and slippers as they entered the low thatched-roof meeting hall called the *mwanieba*. Wanting to honor cultural protocol, we tried following along, copying them. As we ducked our heads under the thatched roof and entered the mwanieba, every eye was fixed on us. I could tell they were curious about us, similar to our previous boat experience when we traveled to North Tarawa. We definitely stood out because we were the only foreigners there.

Everyone gathered in uniform lines inside the large meeting place with the thatched roof above our heads. The service started when one of the pastors came to the front with a raised voice, nearly yelling in the Kiribati language. Though I didn't understand what he was saying, I could tell he was cheerleading everyone to start singing. Just at that moment, I heard an electric synthesizer keyboard rising above the many voices that began singing songs in English. The keyboard sounded boppy and upbeat—fitting for the island, much like you'd hear in the music played on the public transportation vans.

I appreciated that I could connect with the English songs because it was in my language, but I wondered if they understood what it meant. They sang on and went through the motions as though they had sung these songs thousands of times. It was a stylish Pacific twist on our old, mundane worship songs. As spunky and cool as it sounded, though, I wondered if it was worship that came from the heart or just another form of the religious spirit like those I had seen in all the other churches I attended on the island.

Praise and worship ended, and Pastor Katuba began to deliver his sermon. He spoke in the Kiribati language, with a mix of English since Joel and I were there. Despite hearing his occasional English sentences, I still didn't understand what he was preaching about. At the end of the service, Katuba made an alter call. I wondered if this, too, was part of the weekly motions that they went through for each service. However, just at that time I felt a shift in the room.

People began to come to the front and respond to the Lord's presence. Within a moment, the Holy Spirit came in fire and fell on people. Everyone responded in some way. We all began to worship with our hearts open to the Lord. Joel and I got down on our knees in worship. The Lord was ministering in power, without a person directing it. I could tell this wasn't a normal service for them; it was a fresh outpouring of God's love on them. It was purely Him.

This went on for some time, and many people were touched. In my inner man, I could tell what was happening. This was the mark of the Lord, the very fingerprint of God. God marked all of us in that moment, the first time we had ever come together with that church family. It was His stamp of approval, showing us that He brought us together for a reason. I just knew it in my inner man.

BEGINNING A BEAUTIFUL RELATIONSHIP

After all this happened, Katuba called for a meeting with us and all the church leadership. The church wanted to get to know Joel and me better. Unlike the church service where we lined up in rows, we met this time in a large circle inside the mwanieba. This was a traditional way of meeting together, called the Kiribati Protocol. We all positioned ourselves on the ground, cross-legged and in a large circle around the edge of the mwanieba. All the elders of the church looked concerned. I wondered if we did something wrong.

I was uneducated on the cultural protocol for the meeting so I didn't know what would happen. An elder of the church raised his hand. Katuba, who was operating as the emcee, gave him permission to speak. The man quickly stood up with anticipation. Looking at us, he began to ask us questions. "Why are you here? What brought you to our island?" he asked. "Are you connected to an outside church or organization that sent you here?"

As the man voiced his inquiries, many of the elders nodded their heads, showing that they, too, wondered the same thing.

Finishing his questions, he sat down and Katuba looked at me. With my limited exposure to chiefs and tribal leaders, I knew that most indigenous leaders are careful who they let in their community. I assumed that this was the case with the elders of this church. Not knowing exactly what the protocol called for, I raised my hand and asked if I could respond to the elder's questions. Katuba gave me permission as he stood up to translate for me. I also stood, though at a much slower pace in order to gather words in my head. With a deep breath, I began to speak.

"I know you don't know me or my friend here, but we come in peace. My name is Caleb, and my friend is Joel. We are from the USA, and we both have a relationship with Jesus. About one year ago, I was living in Israel, and God spoke to me and told me to come to your islands. I didn't know anything about your country. God made it clear that we are supposed to come here. With much appreciation, my friend, Joel, has also joined me on this trip. Our coming here is a simple act of faith in responding to God's voice. We are not coming under the name of any church or organization. We only come in the name of the Lord Jesus Christ. A few days ago, Pastor Katuba and I met, and I felt like it was a divine connection. Earlier, during our service, the Holy Spirit was so evident in this place that I believe the Lord brought us here for a purpose."

Sitting down and taking up my cross-legged position again, I wondered if my short message was delivered correctly because there was a long silence in the room. Katuba and all the elders began nodding their heads with serious but delighted smiles on their faces.

Katuba stood back up again, just after he had sat down. Clearly, he wanted to say something. With a confident stance, he turned to us and explained, "This kind of responding to God's voice is not well understood in our culture, but we are interested in learning more. We recognize that God has led you here, and we believe today was a sign from God that He has a plan for us to be together. Though we don't know what God's plans are, we want you two to be a part of our community while you are here."

Joel and I were honored, thankful, and pleased to be accepted into this wonderful community of Kiribati believers. We proceeded from the tense meeting to having a delightful lunch with lots of laughter and joy. We had made it through the door of relationship with this church community. Yes, it was nerve-racking at first, but now that we were in, there were great things ahead of us.

As you continue to read on in this book, you'll hear of many miraculous events and evangelistic movements that started because of the relationships that the Lord established on that day between the Kiribati church and us. From that time onward, it seemed that the Lord took us to greater places every time we came together. His presence was the very energy that kept us sustained through that time. All the members of the church, from the old to the young, grew deeper in love and communion with Him. Our community grew in both quality and numbers.

Our only problem was that our scheduled flights out of the country were coming close. I wasn't only leaving these beautiful islands of the Pacific, but Joel and I were also splitting ways. Joel had things to do in the USA, and I was scheduled to go onward to where I felt the Lord leading me.

Taking off in the plane and seeing Tarawa island get smaller and smaller as we flew across the deep blue ocean, I knew it wouldn't be long before I would be coming back. I was marked for Kiribati. For now, though, trusting that the Lord would continue to do what He started in the Kiribati islands, it was time for me to move on. Leaving the islands was not easy, and I had no clue what was in store for me in the coming weeks in a new country I had never been to before: the Philippines.

SIX
THE PHILIPPINES

After our six-week adventure in Kiribati, we left Tarawa island with the grief of leaving the people we had grown so quickly to love. Yet we also had much expectation in our hearts, knowing that we would return.

Joel and I stood in the airport in Sydney, Australia, with tears in our eyes as we said goodbye to each other. We couldn't stop reminiscing about the unimaginable stories that emerged from that short time on those islands.

We also cried because it was time for us to part ways. Joel had prayed and felt that the Lord wanted him to return to America, while I, on the other hand, could not get the Philippines off my mind.

Having spent such a wonderful time with Palu in Israel, I was curious to see if I could catch a flight from Australia to the Philippines that would fit my meager budget. After searching for airline tickets, I found some that I could afford, which only seemed to confirm God's hand in that direction.

I felt like the Philippines was a continuation of the word the Holy Spirit gave me when I was in Israel and He said, "Caleb, I want you to begin to get connected with indigenous people." I felt that the Lord was perhaps calling me to connect with indigenous tribes in the Philippines through my connection with Palu, and although I eagerly wanted Joel to continue to travel with me, the Lord's peace led both of us in our own direction.

When the time came to board, Joel went on his flight to the USA, and I went to my flight, taking me to the main city of the Philippines—Manila. I had no clue what was in store for me for the months ahead. I only knew one person from Manila—a lady named Rachel, whom I had met at the WCGIP. She and her husband, Peter, were kind enough to pick me up at the airport.

I stepped out of the air-conditioned airport into the reality of the tropical climate; it was an awakening greeting to the Philippines. People were bustling around, and everyone was yelling and speaking in languages that I did not understand. I was instantly both impressed and taken aback by the multitudes of people and vehicles congested on a thin, two-laned road.

Standing by the roadside for some time, I instantly recognized a familiar face as soon as I saw it. Rachel, who had a beautiful, motherly smile on her face, rolled down her window and exclaimed, "Welcome to the Philippines!" I hopped in the car with her and her husband, Peter, and we drove to the guest house of Wycliffe Bible Translators.

Peter and Rachel had dedicated their lives to help promote the translation of the Bible into minority language groups. I stayed one week at the Wycliffe Bible Translators' guest house, learning about the process of translating the Word of God into indigenous peoples' languages. I sat at the table with missionaries who have been in the Philippines for decades working on Bible translation for specific people groups. This dedication to have the Word of God translated into many different languages fascinated me. They helped me realize that if the Word of God was not translated into English many years ago, I would not have the opportunity to read the Bible.

More than that, I learned that there were around 170 languages and dialects in the Philippines alone. This was because the Philippine nation is composed of very many islands, so these languages essentially came from each island and from tribal groups that never wanted to blend themselves with other tribal groups. Now that many of the tribal groups are receiving Jesus, they desire to have the Word of God in their language.

FROM THE CITY TO THE JUNGLE

My time at the Wycliffe guest house was wonderful, but more than anything, I was excited to see Palu and Ten again and meet their tribe. They were the ones I really connected with at the WCGIP, and I really felt like God wanted me to be with them. Their tribe was located on an island called Mindanao. Everyone I talked to about Mindanao said, "Don't go there!" It was a very dangerous place due to the Islamic and rebel army strongholds. Many missionaries in the past have been kidnapped and held hostage for ransom. After some prayer about whether or not I should go, I felt the Lord's peace to go. I was aware of the danger, and I did as much research as I could to learn what to do and what not to do.

After many attempts to get in touch with Palu, I finally reached him via phone. His village did not have any signal, so they had to travel to the top of a mountain on a sunny day to get one bar of signal. They call that particular spot "Signal Hill." It was very challenging to understand what he was saying, but through the crackling signal I could hear Palu's voice saying, "I will meet you in Davao City tomorrow with my motorbike."

The next morning, I took a flight down to Mindanao and arrived in the main city of Davao where Palu met me with his motorbike. I was so excited to see him again! We needed to go right away in order to get to his village before it got too late. Traveling at late hours of the night can result in kidnappings or an array of other forms of theft.

Bopping on the back of a small, on/off road motorbike, however, was a difficult drive. Most of the travel was via highway through the mountainous region of Mindanao. Once we got into the region of Palu's tribe, the highways turned into roads, and then finally into small paths that even the motorbikes could barely fit on.

Finally, after six-and-a-half stretched-out hours of hanging onto the back of the motorbike, we arrived in Palu's home village of Iglugsad. Many individuals peeked curiously out of their small bamboo huts as we came rolling in. Some had the courage to meet me in person. I knew that this would be different for them, as some had never seen a foreigner before. None of them could speak English, and I certainly didn't understand anything they said, but we enjoyed each other's smiles. They welcomed me joyfully.

Palu's village was simple. Having recently received electricity, his village was a hub for many other villages that didn't yet have electricity. The people of Palu's tribe, the Manobo, were a very kindhearted people who seemed diligent at their work. They were a reserved and reluctant people, being careful who they conversed with. This could have been due to the long history of tribal war with other indigenous tribes, Muslim tribes, Spanish colonists, and foreigners who attempted to exploit their land. The Manobo were the original people of the mountainous part of Mindanao island. They were farmers and hard workers.

A large river flowed through the village, and many of the bamboo huts and small cinderblock houses sat beside the river. The land was very jungle-like and exotic, with wild animals and large snakes and lizards.

I resided in the village day after day, enjoying every second with this fascinating and enchanting tribe. I was in awe of God's glory that rested on them. They did not associate much with neighboring tribes. Rarely traveling to the city, they only bought essential tools, seeds, and equipment. They would sell their produce to shrewd buyers who would occasionally drive big dump trucks to their village and buy the produce the farmers had at a minimum rate. The buyers would take it back to the city and sell it for a very high price. The tribe was easily taken advantage of, which caused more tension between the tribe and modern society.

Each day was a new adventure for me. I soaked up the culture of the Manobo people, learning all I could about their language, lifestyle, and history. I did a lot of walking around the village and meeting new people each day.

A FRUITFUL MOUNTAIN ADVENTURE

One day some of the villagers asked me if I wanted to climb the mountain to explore. I was thrilled about this. We started hiking up the mountain, picking fruits and tasting them as we went. We got higher and higher up the mountain and I could see how magnificent the mountain range was.

I kept picking fruits and counting them as we hiked. Some of the fruits were large, exotic fruits that I had never seen before. Some were oddly shaped with lots of spikes on them. Some were hard on the outside but soft on the inside. I was reminded of the vast and bountiful blessing God has bestowed on our earth and how thankful I am of the ways the indigenous people have stewarded this blessing through the centuries. We picked more than twenty different kinds of fruits before we got to the top of the mountain.

As we descended the mountain, I held a number of large fruits in my hands. The people who led me were excellent mountain climbers from having grown up near these slopes. I, on the other hand, wasn't as steady, especially with fruits in my hands and flip-flops on my feet. As we approached a dry, steep area, I took more caution. I tried to stay focused but also wanted to impress the tribesmen, proving that this missionary could keep up.

Well, that didn't work. Before I knew it, my foot slipped and I went tumbling down the side of the mountain. Thankfully I stopped myself and was not injured. But to my embarrassment, the fruit I had been gripping in my hands was now bowling down the mountain.

I regained my footing and laughed it off. We slowed our pace and kept descending. After one hour, we arrived near the bottom of the ridge and finally got to some flat land. Walking along the path, we laughed and joked about various things that we saw. And just then, we saw something lying on the path in front of us. It was in the distance, so we couldn't completely see it. Whatever it was, it was certainly not there a few hours before when we went up those trails. We wondered, *Is it a mountain lion or some other dangerous animal?*

As we carefully approached, we realized what the indistinguishable object was: my fruit! I knelt down, picked up the fruit, looked up to God, and said, "Thank you!" Then we proceeded to the village.

WHERE ARE THE INDIGENOUS INSTRUMENTS?

At that time, the people of the Manobo tribe I was staying with were second-generation Christians. In other words, the gospel of Jesus Christ had been shared with the tribe for the first time around thirty years prior to when I was there with them. There were still a handful of villages in this tribe, however, that had not yet heard the gospel. This amounted to thousands of people in their tribe who still needed to hear. When I heard these facts from Palu, my heart dropped, and I felt a great passion to see the fire of God spread through their whole tribe.

One evening, we all gathered in a small wooden church that was built collectively by the tribesmen who had given their lives to Jesus. The sun was setting, and it was dim inside the wooden church building, but we all were excited to gather to worship. I was thrilled to finally hear the sound of their tribe!

As they began to sing what I thought would be ancient tribal sounds, English words struggled off their tongues as they sang old hymns and played a modern acoustic guitar that they bought from the city. Their voices were spectacular, but I didn't understand why they were singing foreign songs. I wondered if they even knew what the English words meant. I, myself, even had a hard time understanding some of the old hymns.

As glorious and worshipful as the English hymns are, they fit best with a certain people and in a certain era. This was certainly *not* the perfect fit. I was curious where their musical instruments were. This tribe had all their cultural practices intact—the way they cooked, their language, their protocols, and their tribal leadership—but where were their musical instruments?

After the service, we all sat together and I asked them, "Where are the musical instruments of your tribe?"

One of the men brightened up when I asked and he replied, "My brother, a long time ago our tribe had instruments that worshiped different gods. But when some of our tribe members gave their life to Jesus, we stopped making instruments because we didn't want to use those old instruments to worship the one true God. It was too difficult for us to hold on to our instruments because every time we saw and heard them, it reminded us of our old way of thinking."

On the last night before I departed, around forty people from different households came to visit me. We all sat in a circle. One of the tribal leaders shared his appreciation for my visit. In that moment, he started to cry uncontrollably. It was the Lord's tears. It spread to nearly everyone in the room, including me. It wasn't necessarily that we were sad or that something was wrong; the tears came from the knowledge that God had truly brought us together and His love filled our hearts with a deep sense of community.

The next morning, I strapped my few raggedy bags to the back of the motorbike and the tribesmen gathered around me with sad faces. I prayed a prayer that came out of the depths of my inner man, saying, "Lord, if you want me to come back, make it clear when and how."

I left the Manobo tribe and started my journey back to the USA. It was a long series of flights that gave me ample time to think and process. I was excited about all the things that unfolded during my exposure to the Kiribati and Philippine islands, but what was next?

As you learn to follow God's voice, you will sometimes have the same question. I've heard it said that the Bible promises God's Word is a lamp to our feet, meaning that sometimes we can only see the next step, but nothing more. Hearing stories like this one can make people think, *Oh, look at all the amazing things that happened! God speaks to them so clearly. They always know what to do.* No, I very much do not always know what to do. Neither will you. But God is good, and He will always give us the guidance we need as we just keep taking steps forward to follow Him.

As evidence of this, I didn't know yet that the months ahead held a series of events that would mold and shape me to be the person God needed me to be. It wouldn't be my choice of events, but God certainly used the next season to reveal my heart by refining me. The questions would be, Was I willing to be shaped? Was I willing to endure the refinement?

SEVEN
OBEDIENCE

Thoughts, prayers, and emotions hit me over and over as I sat on my narrow middle seat of the plane. I murmured a simple prayer while I contemplated all these things: "My Leader, I heard a word from You to go to these islands and connect with indigenous people, and now I've responded to that word. Here I am. I have seen your glory manifested as I responded. But there has to be more than this. What is it? What's next?"

Just then I heard a direct word from the Father that penetrated my soul. He said, "My son, will you live your life wholeheartedly for me?"

I heard those words so strongly from the Lord. They weren't audible, but they rang inside my heart loud and clear. As if it was a no-brainer, I quickly replied to the Lord saying, "Father, you know I will live for you wholeheartedly!"

Then, just like that, I didn't hear anything. It was an intentional silence from God to make me take what He asked seriously. I frantically searched my heart, wondering, *Am I really willing to live for Him with all my heart?*

Without a clear answer from the Lord, and being unable to

OBEDIENCE

fully know my own heart, I thought, *Perhaps the Lord is inviting me into a season of learning obedience on a deeper level.* I wasn't sure what this would look like, but I felt the joyful invitation of the Father, almost as if He was telling me, *Son, come with Me. I have some things to teach you.*

When I got home, it was encouraging to be back with my family and friends again. I had stories to share. My home church embraced me and graciously allowed me to share my missionary exposure testimonies with them. The more that I told stories, however, the more my heart longed to go back.

One sunny spring day I was strolling down a well-beaten path at a local park. I often went on walks when I needed to process life's trajectory, and this was one of those times.

As much as I loved being home, I yearned to be back in the nations with the tribes. I was running into one major issue with my life, however, and that was money. My bank account was empty, I walked around in flip-flops, I didn't have a car, and I lived in my parents' basement. The most logical thing for me to do was get a job.

As I strolled along the scenic greenway, the voice of the Lord came to me again saying, "Caleb, go to the creek. I want to speak to you through the water."

There was a creek nearby, so I veered off the path and trekked through the woods over to the small creek. When I arrived there, I knelt down and took off my flip-flops as I felt God's manifest presence again. This time I was geared for His voice, knowing He was going to speak; I just didn't know what He would say. I leaned down and listened to the water as it trickled through the stones, my attention on the Lord. All of a sudden, I heard Him through the water. This is what He said: "Caleb, I want you to build seven instruments with your friend Michael. As you build them, I will speak to you again."

Then a great joy came over me. I was filled with joy like I had never been before. I ran around the greenway, jumping with joy in God's presence. I didn't understand the word, but that didn't matter right then. I realized that what mattered was His love. I knew there was purpose in His words, even with my limited understanding. I quickly called Michael, who was one of my best friends. I shared with him the word I heard from the Lord, and he was also overcome with the Father's joy as I spoke it.

Now, I know you're probably thinking, *This Caleb is a wacko! How can he hear God's voice through water?* I understand why that might sound wacko, but I'm telling you, God can use nature to display His will in whatever ways He wants. The Lord called Moses from within a burning bush, God used a donkey to talk to Balaam, and He appointed a great fish to swallow up Jonah. While it's maybe not the most common way He speaks to people, there's many examples from the Bible to show He definitely could speak to me (or anyone) through water. What is true for certain is that He absolutely desires His children to hear what He's saying, no matter how He says it to them.

TRUST, THEN UNDERSTAND

The word the Lord gave me that day catapulted me into an incredible season of creativity, and Michael was excited to join me on this journey. Through prayer and waiting, we began to get more clarity from the Holy Spirit. We felt that God wasn't asking for any specific type of instruments, but that He was inviting us into a process of creativity that we had not tapped into before. It was clear, too, that God didn't want a specific product; rather, He wanted the process. I didn't understand the why for all this, but I embraced the reality that it's okay to not understand and obey anyway.

Michael was a guitar player and I was a drummer, so we quickly came up with a game plan on what instruments we would make. There was much enthusiasm as we sketched our list of instruments on a small piece of paper: rattling shaker, Djembe drum, boat lute, two-stringed Asian style violin, Native American style flute, Shakuhachi flute, and a rain stick. We gathered all of the materials together and asked my dad if we could borrow a corner of his furniture-making shop for our dedicated instrument-making location. My dad let us use it and was wildly excited to do it.

We pretty much struggled through the whole process. There was a lot to learn on many levels, but thankfully, our church community had professional woodworkers and metal smiths who were willing to answer any questions we had. A highly skilled woodworker offered us lessons two times a week, giving us practical skills on how to work with each material. Each instrument was a wonderfully challenging process. We learned a variety of skills, especially concerning the vast amount of qualities God placed inside each material we used.

As we ventured through this process, we learned that God's purpose wasn't necessarily about making the instruments; it was more about the process of obedience. It was about the process of hearing and doing what we thought the Lord was saying. It was also about partnering with Jesus in everything in life, including splitting, planing, and sanding wood. It was a joyful process even though there were many failures. I broke costly materials and got angry on some days. Every day, Michael and I messed up in some way. We didn't get it all right, but that's exactly where the Lord wanted us to be because, again, this was about our hearts.

We completed the seven instruments. They were not the greatest-sounding instruments. They didn't look all that beautiful, either, but that didn't matter. What we learned through the process was invaluable. I gained a fascination for sounds and a desire to see instruments from every tribe and nation used for God's glory. A seed was deposited in me. I was reminded of that day in Kiribati when I heard the boppy keyboard music and

English hymns. I remembered that night in the Philippines when I heard the foreign guitar and the tribesmen straining to sing English songs. Something clicked in me, and I realized that God made me to be both a musician and craftsmen for a reason.

Around that time, Palu from the Philippines called me. He and Ten were able to call from Signal Hill. I could barely hear him through the choppy signal, but it was a delight to hear his voice again. As we talked, Palu said, "Can you come back to the Philippines? We need your help."

"What's wrong?" I asked. "How can I help?"

"We want to redeem our musical instruments so that we can worship God with our own sound. I know you are a musician, and you can make things. Maybe you can help us make our instruments so we can worship with our own sound?"

I was amazed! This was why God wanted me to make the seven instruments! This was why He took me through the whole process of learning, so I could help redeem the sounds of worship in this tribe. I just knew for certain that this was God, so right there on the phone, I told Palu that I would be back in the Philippines in a few months.

LIVE WITH GOD—WHOLEHEARTEDLY

Around that time, I was studying the book of Deuteronomy. In the first few chapters, it explains how Moses and all of the Israelites, after their forty-year journey through the desert, finally reached a ridge called Moab where they saw the Promised Land in front of them. Moses addresses Israel there, saying,

> Now this is the commandment—the statutes and the rules—that the LORD your God commanded me to teach you, that you may do them in the land to which you are going over, to

possess it, that you may fear the LORD your God, you and your son and your son's son, by keeping all his statutes and his commandments, which I command you, all the days of your life, and that your days may be long. Hear therefore, O Israel, and be careful to do them, that it may go well with you, and that you may multiply greatly, as the LORD, the God of your fathers, has promised you, in a land flowing with milk and honey.

Hear, O Israel: The LORD our God, the LORD is one. You shall love the LORD your God with all your heart and with all your soul and with all your might. And these words that I command you today shall be on your heart. You shall teach them diligently to your children, and shall talk of them when you sit in your house, and when you walk by the way, and when you lie down, and when you rise. You shall bind them as a sign on your hand, and they shall be as frontlets between your eyes. You shall write them on the doorposts of your house and on your gates. (Deuteronomy 6:1–9)

I had read these Scripture verses over and over again as a child, but at that moment on that chilly November morning, I read these verses and I knew that God was calling me to my own Promised Land and a covenant with Him. The covenant was that I would live a life of obedience to Him, and in return He would bless my steps and give me the nations. I knew in my heart that the Father was inviting me into fellowship with Jesus Christ and His finished work. This wasn't a covenant of works, but a covenant of obedience within a faith in the finished work of Christ. The Lord Himself was drawing me into communion with Him. He gently reminded me of what He asked me months before on that plane ride, "Will you live your life wholeheartedly for Me?"

I had given my life to Jesus as a child, and I already knew that my eternal life with Him was secured. But what God was saying to me was related to here and now, on earth. The Lord was asking for everything—my desires, my plans, my hopes, my future, my everything.

In essence, God was saying, "You're shifting from living *for* me to living *with* me. Let's do life together."

I had so much joy about it because I knew His love was all I needed. I knew that the Father was calling me to a Promised Land, but it required me to be a lightweight to get there, meaning that I couldn't be carrying emotional, possessional, or mental baggage with me. That's what the obedience was about—being free to go and do His will.

That afternoon, I stepped into my parents' kitchen and scanned the countertop for a quick snack. There was a basket of grapes sitting there. I walked up to it and was fascinated as I gazed at the basket. They were the largest grapes I had ever seen in my life. I knew immediately that it was a sign from God, sealing His covenant with me. Just as spies went to the Promised Land and came back with a cluster of grapes, I knew God was showing me that it was for me too.

A SURPRISE INTERRUPTION

A few days after that life-changing moment, something bizarre happened. It was a frigid Thursday evening, and I came home from a long day's work in the shop. I fell into a deep sleep around 10:00 p.m. to get rest for another big day's work. Around 11:30 p.m., however, I woke up with an immense pain in my chest. It was an intense throbbing pain that surrounded my whole chest with striking jabs every minute. I tried rolling around to relieve the pain, but it would not leave.

Upon realizing the seriousness of what was happening to my body, I managed to roll myself out of bed. I staggered and stumbled, trying desperately to make my way upstairs, feeling the pain increase the farther I got. Each step was a struggle.

I staggered into my parents' room. Of course, they were still sleeping, but, hearing me struggling, my mom quickly awoke and asked, "Caleb, what's wrong?"

Trying to find my voice, I mumbled, "My chest hurts."

Both my parents rose immediately from their sleep.

Just at that moment, something "coincidentally" happened to both of them. A thick, dark wave of sickness swept over them and they were immediately sick. They both fell back into their bed and felt paralyzed in that position. I fell on their bed, too, with increasing chest pain. It seemed choking and paralyzing.

Unable to help myself, I started falling into a deep tunnel of darkness, feeling like everything was caving in on me. My dad finally exerted enough strength to get out of bed. He managed to assist me to his car and rush me to the hospital.

I stumbled into the emergency room, unable to breathe well, and the doctors quickly checked me. Seeing the seriousness of my condition, they put me in critical care. I was treated urgently by a caring doctor and before too long, my heart rate went back down. I was able to get a room to stay in the hospital.

After four long days of recovery in the hospital, the doctors came to explain what happened to me. Though they don't know where it came from, the doctors said that there was inflammation and liquid around my heart, something called pericarditis. They ordered me to rest for ten weeks. For a twenty-two-year-old man, that was hard, but I followed the doctor's orders. I needed to get better so I could get back to the Philippines.

I didn't understand exactly why this happened to me. When things like this happen, it's easy to ask, "Did God do this, or did Satan do it?" It was difficult to think that God would do such a thing to people. On the other hand, if God allowed Satan to do it, what about the finished work of Christ? Why would a thing like this happen to me when I was on such a beautiful trajectory of hearing God's voice and responding to Him?

It's true that these questions swirled in my mind during those ten weeks, but I made up my mind to not spend my energy trying to figure it out. Instead, I put my energy into believing that God would turn it into something good. I made up my mind that, just like making those seven instruments, this was a matter of the heart, of learning to trust Him. I was determined to believe that God was going to take care of me no matter what. I knew that in my weakness, His strength was going to be made perfect.

I took it easy and went slowly, and I didn't do anything strenuous. I followed the doctor's orders to not pick up anything heavier than ten pounds. Each week I got better and better, and I looked forward to going back to the doctor for my ten-week checkup.

THE SURPRISES KEEP COMING

That moment came along with an abrupt surprise. For some odd reason, my heart started reverting to the pain I had felt at first. Every time I bent down, an intense and sharp jab would strike my chest. I didn't understand what was happening. I was literally two days away from my final checkup and the tables turned. In agony and concern, I contacted my doctor to request an early checkup.

After the results were available, the doctor explained that he saw damaged tissue around my heart. I was discouraged to hear that. He said that he needed to get more testing done in order to diagnose my condition, so he scheduled me for an MRI.

The doctor explained that I needed to be still inside the MRI in order for the scan to work properly, then they placed me on the MRI table, and I went inside. Lying inside the large spaceship-looking scanner, I focused all my attention on being fixed as soon as possible.

This was easier said than done, but after about an hour of waiting inside the big machine, something happened. In just a moment, like a changing scene in a movie, I felt the manifest presence of Jesus come into the MRI with me. Though there was not much extra space inside the spaceship bed, Jesus was inside it too. Feeling shocked, I asked Him, *Jesus, why are You in here?*

Immediately, I entered into a vision. In the vision, I stood in an empty room with only Jesus standing about eight feet in front of me. He faced me directly and started walking toward me. All I could feel was love as I stared into His fiery eyes. He approached me slowly but with confidence, and placed His hand on my heart. With tender, bold words, He announced, "Caleb, I've created you for a specific purpose." Then His hand lifted, moving from my heart to my shoulder. As His hand rested on my shoulder, I could feel a surge of energy flow through my body. Then the vision ended.

It was powerful. I felt as if I could jump ecstatically out of the MRI. Not very long after that, the siren went off, indicating the scanning session was over. The nurses came into the room, just as if it had been an ordinary MRI, to assist me out of the machine. Then the doctor entered the room, looking a bit shocked. He held the scans in his hand and, with an astonished look on his face, he said, "Well, I expected there to be damaged tissue just like our last results. However, as you can see, there is absolutely no damage at all. In fact, your heart looks brand new. If any doctor were to ever look at your heart, they wouldn't be able to tell anything ever happened."

It was an amazing miracle. I walked out of the hospital that day with tears flowing down my face. I had seen the face of Jesus, was commissioned by His grace, and He healed my heart. Honestly, whether He healed my heart or gave me a new heart, I don't know. What I did know was that I was filled with joy because I was now clear to go to the Philippines! The doctor gave me the green light. Miraculously, I had no more pain in my heart from that day onward.

I learned much during that time of my life. That season of walking out the Lord's calling in the midst of sickness, hardship, and many questions was clearly a mark of the Lord to prepare me for a life of obedience.

From that day on, my focus was on the bullseye. All my energy, funding, and vision went into my preparation for living among the unreached people groups. I started training my body to live in the elements of the jungle by sleeping on the hard ground at night. I saved as much funds as I could by living as frugally as I could.

I knew that extraordinary things were ahead because I knew this was God's plan. I knew that if God calls, God supplies. God's provision proceeds His commission. I knew that I just needed to step out in obedience and walk it out despite the curveballs life sometimes throws at us. I needed to learn the art of rolling with the punches by trusting God—not with my own strength, but with His. After months of preparing myself physically, mentally, spiritually, and in my craftsmanship, I was ready for this assignment.

EIGHT
REDEEMING THE ANCIENT SOUNDS

I was ready! That fact alone filled me with joy. I had certainly needed the season of preparation that the Holy Spirit took me through, but now I was deeply excited to return to the Philippines. This time, I would go with a mission and on a one-way ticket, not knowing exactly how long I would be gone.

Thankfully, my friend, Michael, who helped me build the seven instruments, traveled with me for the first month. He had a brilliant engineering mind, having studied mechanical engineering at a university. We created a strategic plan for executing what we needed to do to get the instruments made.

Before you can make instruments, you have to have tools. Before you have tools, you have to make tools to make those tools. And not just that, but you have to have a place to store all of the tools where you can also work with those tools, and have a safe environment for the instruments to be protected without being exposed to the elements. Our general plan was to build a shop, make tools that could make tools, collect wood and materials from the forest for the instruments, make the tools that would eventually make the instruments, and then—last but not least—make the instruments.

Arriving in the Philippines, we wasted no time and traveled directly to Mindanao. Getting back with the Manobo tribe was fulfilling and thrilling. It was a joy to introduce them to Michael and for us to get integrated into the tribal life again. Even though we had a specific assignment from the Lord, we didn't push it too hard. As much as the assignment was needed, relationship with the people was even more important, and relationship requires time.

One of the key tools to learn in life is this: learn how to walk in the pace of the *Lord* and the *land*. If we came to the tribe with a rush to fulfill our mission, we would miss the whole point. If we pushed too hard, it would make the tribe feel like we were forcing an agenda on them, and that's not what we wanted to do. We wanted to bless them and see this ultimately as God's kingdom growing among them as a people. This could only come if we learned the pace of the Lord *and* the land.

Michael and I trekked up to the gathering hall where all the tribal chieftains sat in a circle discussing something. With welcoming smiles, they invited us into their gathering to tell them more about the instrument-making venture. Palu stood with us to communicate and explain why we were there and what our plans were. To my surprise, the chiefs were thrilled to receive us into their community; in fact, they already knew we were coming due to Palu preparing for our arrival. This was good because we were aware of the protocol that was needed for entering the tribe. This, too, was a key tool for missions: always find the man of peace. Palu was our man of peace. Without him, we would not have been able to integrate into the community with peace.

> "Whatever house you enter, first say, 'Peace be to this house!'
> And if a son of peace is there, your peace will rest upon him.

But if not, it will return to you. And remain in the same house, eating and drinking what they provide, for the laborer deserves his wages." (Luke 10:5–7)

The good news is that the tribe was completely ready to jump into the process of making instruments. They had already made plans for our arrival, and the families were ready for whatever was needed. We formed a group of ten men who would be the instrument makers. Most of these men were believers and they had already obtained some teaching about God's love, but they were hungry for discipleship—to grow in the Lord and to encounter His love. My desire was to use the instrument-making process as a safe place of discipleship. This would be the place where we could all learn, love, and grow through the curveballs that life throws at us.

OUR FIRST SETBACK

Our plan was to first build the workshop where we would make the instruments. The location was given to us by one of the believers, and we were deeply grateful. It was a perfect place in the middle of the village. The only problem was that there was a seventy-foot-high coconut tree directly in the middle of where we wanted to build our workshop. Our plan was to cut the tree, mill it into lumber, and use the lumber to build our shop. The challenge with that plan was that there was not a good spot to drop it, as there were small houses all around the tree.

After the word got around about what we were doing, a man appeared with a large chainsaw. He casually walked up with a hand-rolled cigarette in his mouth, wearing shorts and flip-flops. He leaned against the tree and, with a confident look on his face, said he was an experienced chainsaw operator. We were reluctant, but it was our only option besides chopping the tree down with an axe.

There was only one spot where the tree could be dropped—about a twenty-foot gap between two small houses. The man with the chainsaw didn't talk much as he prepared his tools for dropping the tree. We did our part and quickly got all the people and valuable items out of the way. With his cigarette still in his mouth and the chainsaw in his hands, he eye-balled where to drop the tree and started cutting. He cut a notch on one side of the tree where he wanted it to drop. Looking at the notch, I could already tell that this wasn't going where it was supposed to go. It wasn't just me either. Everyone in our group kept tilting our heads to the side, wondering what this man was doing.

He then went to the side opposite of the notched-out section and cut diagonally straight over to the notch. The internal tree fibers started popping as the gigantic tree started leaning in one direction. In a flash, it came barreling down.

At that point, we had no control over the tree. It would drop where it would drop. The problem is that it was going the wrong direction!

We all saw it tumbling directly toward the neighbor's house. A rush of fear came over all of us. Was everyone out of the house that was about to get smashed? Were there valuable belongings in there? Before anyone could even let out a yell, the damage was done. What had once been home to a Manobo farming family was now a pile of broken boards and bashed belongings.

Quickly scanning through the multitudes of wide-eyed spectators who stood at a distance, we saw the parents and children of the family who owned the home. A deep sense of relief swept over us as we realized no one had been inside. Thank God! We ran over to them, apologizing for destroying their bamboo home full of all their possessions.

Everyone then turned their heads toward the chainsaw man

who still had his pitiful, stubby cigarette in his mouth, puffing away like it wasn't his fault. Even though it was his fault in the sense that he was the person who cut the tree, we knew it was also our fault because we let him do the job, and a sense of failure came over all of us as we stared at the coconut tree on top of the house and wood shattered everywhere. My financial weight for this project didn't just double, but what we had to build doubled too. Not just that, but now we had the responsibility to care for this family since they didn't have a home to live in.

We had only just started our work, and we were already faced with a crushing setback—literally. The work ahead of us was daunting, but we reminded ourselves that we were doing this with God's help. We knew right away that in order to accomplish this assignment of redeeming the instruments of worship, we absolutely must partner with the Holy Spirit. Jesus said that His yoke is easy and His burden is light. If we didn't grasp the reality of God's goodness, we would be striving through the whole thing, never to see the true fruit of God's grace. This is what Michael and I preached over and over again to the tribespeople who worked with us, and it's a necessary lesson for anyone who wants to follow God's voice.

BEGINNING TO BUILD MOMENTUM

The days, weeks, and months ahead were full of hard work, worship, prayer, counseling, and scratching our heads as we tried to figure out how things worked. Every day was a challenge, but we kept moving forward and won victories. One early victory was that Michael helped me invent a bike-powered grinder. This grinder came in handy, as we were making all sorts of high-carbon steel tools for the instruments. More victories came as the shop was built, and then the neighbor's house was rebuilt much better than it was before. After that we focused on building tools that would be used for making instruments.

After some time, Michael went back to the United States. We knew the Lord brought him there for a season for a special reason, but now his assignment with us was finished. I was sad to see him go, but I knew that the Holy Spirit would give me strength to continue by myself.

Six long months later, we finally finished the shop and all the tools. The shop was fully equipped now with all we needed to build nearly any type of musical instrument by hand.

Our next step was to all gather together to get wisdom from the chiefs of the tribe. We wanted to discuss how we should proceed from that point. The chiefs began by telling us they were impressed with how we had gotten so far already. Even that much progress was truly a glorious picture of how God brings people together to bring life.

The instrument makers and I asked the chiefs and elders of the tribe what their instruments were like when they were young. We all quieted ourselves, leaning in to hear the elders' voices quietly tell tales of their childhood. They told us fragmented stories of the instruments they remembered. I held a notepad in my hand as they explained what their instruments were like, what kind of materials they were made of, and how they sounded. I jotted down as much information as possible, and though it was very fragmented information, it was enough to give us mental visuals of the instruments they use to play in the tribe. We collected enough information for two different types of drums, two types of flutes, a two-stringed lute, shakers, and a xylophone made of bamboo poles called knocking blocks.

Once we knew what we were going to make, we needed to figure out how to make it. Having only basic hand tools and a jungle of materials, we leaned on the Holy Spirit for creativity and innovation. After some planning and discussion, we made a schedule for who would work at what times. The ten instrument makers split up into groups that would come on different days of the week. I worked every day and with each group, helping to teach hand techniques and how to use the tools.

This teaching process was always an adventure. As much as I'd love to say that I knew what I was doing, I didn't! I was learning as I was teaching.

We started each day with prayer and worship. Many days, we would stop in the middle of our work to talk about something in the Bible or about the goodness of God. On some days, the instrument makers had issues that we needed to work through. It was truly a magnificent experience of working and living in communion with each other and with God.

Acquiring the materials we needed for the instruments was not always an easy task. Our first journey into the forest required an hour of hiking up a mountain to find a large mahogany tree. After cutting it down with an axe, we sectioned it into three-foot lengths with a two-man handsaw, and then hauled each piece on our shoulders down the mountain, which included crossing a river to get back to the village. This required an immense amount of determination, strength, and balance.

HARD STEPS IN DISCIPLESHIP

Another time, we searched for a mango tree because it is a softer wood that has a good resonant quality. We looked far and wide but were not able to find one.

That week a powerful tropical storm came through the area. As we huddled together under Palu's roof, lightning kept striking all around us. The next morning, as everyone in the village peeked their heads out of their huts and assessed the storm damage, a young boy came running to us. He exclaimed,

"A mango tree, a mango tree!" and was pointing at a large field nearby. As we squinted to look where he was pointing, we could see a gigantic tree that had been struck by lightning the previous night.

The owners of the property offered to give the tree to us. I was thrilled about it, knowing that it was a gift from God. The instrument makers, however, were not so excited about it. I asked them why and they said that according to their tradition, when lightning strikes a tree, the tree becomes cursed. If you cut into the wood that has been struck by lightning, the curse will come down upon you.

I went to my prayer closet about this and asked the Lord what we should do about it. The Lord reminded me of this Scripture passage:

> For everything created by God is good, and nothing is to be rejected if it is received with thanksgiving, for it is made holy by the word of God and prayer. If you put these things before the brothers, you will be a good servant of Christ Jesus, being trained in the words of the faith and of the good doctrine that you have followed. Have nothing to do with irreverent, silly myths. Rather train yourself for godliness. (1 Timothy 4:4–7)

I felt like God blessed us with that mango tree, and I knew from this Scripture that if we received it with thanksgiving then God would protect us and it would be used for His glory. This wasn't the easiest truth to convey to them since this was deeply woven into their culture and belief system. If they chose to cut into the wood, the whole village would watch and accuse them of leaving their cultural ways. They were genuinely afraid of the tree because this fear was passed on to them through the generations.

While they were afraid of the tree itself, I was afraid of confronting them about their fear. This meant that I had to confront my own fear even as I challenged them to confront their fears. It was a challenge for all of us to face our fears, and it took guts.

On Saturday and Sunday as we rested and worshiped together, I talked a lot about what 1 Timothy 4 meant. Though the apostle Paul wasn't writing to Timothy about mango trees, he was trying to make the point that many people have departed from the truth that all things created by God are blessed. I knew this would be a great opportunity to show them that, even though they are Manobo people, when they give their lives to Jesus they are adopted into the family of God. Being in this new family means they must let go of their old cultural ways that don't line up with God's truth and receive the new culture of heaven. We should all do that, no matter what culture we are from.

The kingdom way of thinking about the tree is to see it as a blessing and not a curse. After some discussion and prayer, they acknowledged that it is a blessing from God. They started to face the tree through the lens of the blood of Christ. They were confident that when Christ died on the cross, His work was finished. As Peter wrote, "His divine power has granted to us all things that pertain to life and godliness, through the knowledge of him who called us to his own glory and excellence" (2 Peter 1:3).

After a week, they approached me as I was getting up in the morning, explaining that they had already prepared axes and saws for cutting up the tree. We sectioned off three-foot lengths for drums and five-foot lengths for two-stringed lutes. We finally had the wood we needed.

A MUSICAL PARTNERSHIP WITH HOLY SPIRIT

We brought all the materials together to begin our carving. The tools that we fashioned were put to great use. We first carved out the two-foot log sections from the inside, carving the internal diameter of the drum. Then we shaped the outside to match the contour of the inside. The instrument makers grew skillful quickly due to their many years of using the *bolo* (machete). They only needed simple guidance to know how to use the tools they had never used before. Within a few hours, each person was well on their way to making their instruments out of the stunning mango wood.

The women and kids helped too. The kids sat at the feet of their fathers and pretended to be making their own musical instruments. They also helped pass tools around. The women and other tribesmen cooked and assisted with various other tasks.

Day by day, we got closer and closer. We were learning as we went since we didn't have someone to show us how the instruments were made. Each instrument required a different process. We used our creativity and intuition to get where we needed to go. I've said it before, but it bears repeating: it was a beautiful partnership between us and the Holy Spirit.

There was much excitement in the air as the instruments started coming together. Seeing these different materials from the forest starting to make actual sound was thrilling.

Even in this wonderful scene of seeing the redemption of these instruments, the tribesmen didn't want to play them until they were all completely finished. This was because they wanted all the instruments to be dedicated to the one true God at the same time. They wanted the instruments to glorify Him and only Him, so once we finished an instrument, we set it to the side until all of them were finished.

We completed first the bamboo flutes, then we proceeded with the drums, then the two-stringed boat lutes, and then finished with the shakers and bamboo xylophone. All the instruments made different sounds and were unique. As a musician, I could already hear them in my head. Profound anticipation welled up in me to hear them all together.

DEDICATING THE INSTRUMENTS AT LAST

Finally, after nearly a year of labor we completed all of the instruments. An array of musical instruments filled the workshop floor. Some were stacked on top of each other. Gazing upon the instruments gave us a deep sense of gratitude. Though they were not successful in a worldly viewpoint—there was no money or fame attached to them—they carried a beautiful story of redemption. This story included the blood, sweat, and tears of building the shop; the many conversations with the chiefs to collect information about the ancient instruments; the strenuous hikes and treks into the forest to collect materials; the decisions that defined who we were as citizens of heaven; the tools we learned to use; the team we formed; and ultimately, the sound of worship that was to be released unto the one true God.

That Sunday morning, we collected all the instruments together and brought them to the church building. Everyone started coming to the church, even people we had never seen before. The wooden pews were filled until people stood on the outside of the church, looking through the wooden window slats. There were chiefs and leaders wearing all of their tribal clothing. Many people traveled from far away to attend this special gathering.

After the elders calmed the crowd, they explained what the day was all about. The chief told the whole story of how they wanted their ancient musical instruments to be redeemed back to Manama (God). The service started with prayer to honor God and dedicate the instruments of worship, then we proceeded with playing music unto Him.

The melodies, harmonies, and rhythms created a beautifully unique sound that reawakened the ancient Manobo music. The music filled the wooden church building and echoed through the mountain range. Those from the village could hear the sound. Many of the tribesmen joined in by dancing and shouting unto the Lord. Before we knew it, we were all caught up in a glorious wind of worship and His presence. The Lord met us as we poured out our love to Him. It was perhaps the purest Manobo form of worship that had been released up until that point. My heart leaped with joy as I watched them all dance and worship.

An old woman who was part of the chief's family came up to me in tears. Her eyes were filled with joy. Over the loud rhythms of the drums, she leaned in emotionally and shouted in my ears, "I have not heard this sound since I was a young child!"

I believe ancient strongholds broke in the atmosphere that day when the ancient sound of worship was reawakened—a sound that was true to the heart of the Manobo people. It was a glorious sound that ushered in the Lord.

> Lift up your heads, O gates! And be lifted up, O ancient doors, that the King of glory may come in. Who is this King of glory? The Lord, strong and mighty, the Lord, mighty in battle! Lift up your heads, O gates! And lift them up, O ancient doors, that the King of glory may come in. Who is this King of glory? The Lord of hosts, he is the King of glory! Selah. (Psalm 24:7–10)

THE SHIFT

From that day onward, there was a shift in the spiritual realm for this tribe. The tribe had their sound. It wasn't just a musical sound; it was *their* spiritual sound. This vibration could only come from the Lord, and it would be transformational for the unreached people in their neighboring tribes in the days and years ahead. An abundance of kingdom harvest started unfolding from that day onward for the Manobo and their neighboring tribes.

NINE
A BOY NAMED JUVY

It had been four years since I left home, following the Lord's leading to Israel, and shortly after that, to Kiribati and then the Philippines. I was only twenty-four years old at this time, and while I had already spent significant time overseas, all my experiences were still pioneering a new dimension in my life. After all, I had spent my entire childhood living in a small town in North Carolina, never even dreaming about this kind of life!

With all that in mind, you can understand how receiving a package from my parents was like finding a lost treasure. In the midst of all the hard work of instrument-making among the Manobo tribe, a notification arrived that a package was waiting for me in the city. I quickly hopped on a motorbike to drive to the city and receive my package. The beat-up cardboard box looked like it had been dragged by a rope attached to the tail of a fox being chased by a hound dog all the way from the United States to the Philippines. I wondered if anything still existed inside and expected to be a bit disappointed.

To my surprise, it was the opposite when I opened it. I could smell home. Tears of sadness but thankfulness flowed down as I picked up letters from my parents and siblings and read through them. Being a missionary who didn't have a supporting organization wasn't easy. I loved hearing God's voice and responding to it, which was why I was there, but it came with a price—a big price—and what I fought more than anything was loneliness.

In addition to the personal notes from home, there, smashed up in the corner of the box, was my favorite childhood snack—Swiss Cake Rolls. Relief that it made it all the way there added to my sense of excitement. I had gone months without any chocolate or comfort foods, so this simple snack that I would normally pass by at home became my comfort and taste of home. Every day, after a hard day's work, I would sneak back to my room and have a few bites of the snack.

Or at least I did until one dreadful night when, in the wee hours of the night while all the tribe slept, I was awakened by a crackling sound. Fresh from the depths of my sleep, I wondered if I was dreaming, and I forced my eyes open against their will, as it were.

I focused my attention on the crackling sound just above my suitcase, and there it was: the silhouette of a monster-like rat hovering over my Swiss Cake Rolls. I had dealt with this issue previously in Kiribati when a rat kept getting into my food, but this wasn't a normal rat; this was a monster rat. It was nearly the size of a cat and had an ugly long tail that flapped confidently back and forth like a whip.

I didn't care what it was, though; nothing was going to mess with my Swiss Cake Rolls. I slowly crept out of bed in stealth mode and grabbed my towel from the table. I rolled it up, turning it into a baseball-bat-like object. Then, pouncing, I swung my "bat" and knocked that rat out of the house. I felt like I hit a homerun as I listened to the rat scatter fearfully away.

Grateful for my victory over the monster, I turned and saw that my box of snacks was ruined. There was, however, one fragment of my Swiss Cake Roll still intact and untouched by the strange jungle creature. I'm not going to say whether I had a midnight rat-eaten snack or not. The important thing to take note of is that the rat never came back, and I'm still alive.

Such were the days and nights of a missionary's life in the remote jungle. It wasn't always the exhilaration of knocking rats out of the baseball field though. It took a lot of consistent hard work and unconditional love in the midst of opposition. I was always reminded of Jesus's words that many have taken refuge in:

> "Come to me, all who labor and are heavy laden, and I will give you rest. Take my yoke upon you, and learn from me, for I am gentle and lowly in heart, and you will find rest for your souls. For my yoke is easy, and my burden is light." (Matthew 11:28–30)

The yoke of the Lord is a double yoke, meaning that we are only to co-labor with Him in His work. It's not our work, but His. It's not our ministry, but His. There were days when I felt like I was carrying it by myself, and on those days, I would be quiet before Him and He would remind me that He's with me.

ONE FACE OF DISCIPLESHIP

We continued to build instruments with the Manobo tribe. Once we were finished with the initial hard work, we shifted into more of a ministry to bring in people to work with us and be discipled in the process. Many of the tribesmen were able to learn craftsmanship skills while also growing in the Lord.

During that time, there was a little boy named Juvy who came on the scene. When I first saw him, he had the appearance of a ten-year-old, but he was actually fifteen. I was told that his growth was stunted due to a bad horse bite. Juvy roamed from place to place because he didn't have a family. At times, he was found sleeping on the cold ground without shelter. He became nomadic at a young age and would go around asking if people needed help in their cornfields or pig pens. He would work in exchange for a place to stay.

He came to us one day asking for work. We happily welcomed him to live with us and assist us in building instruments. Every day we would spend hours working on drums and flutes as we talked and laughed together. We could see that he was happy to finally have a warm home to stay in and people to interact with. He asked many questions and observed our lifestyle of family, but always kept quiet about himself.

One night as we were having dinner, he began telling us things about his life. They shocked us. He told us his story of rejection, of never being accepted in homes, including his father's home. We stopped eating just to listen to him tell his sorrowful history. As he was finishing his sad story, he simply said, "And after I die, I know where I'm going, the place where I deserve to go—hell."

Palu, sitting opposite from Juvy at the table, objected, "No, you are welcomed into the family of God, and it's free for you!"

Juvy replied, "That family is for you, but I have no education, no parents, no money, and no life. It's obvious where I'm destined to go."

Palu spoke up, explaining the goodness of God to him in their own language. He talked for a long time, telling Juvy about what Jesus did for him and how he is loved and cherished by God. This was the first time Juvy had ever heard the Good News.

When Palu finished, the room grew silent as Juvy focused his attention on the table, searching for words to say. Just then, the Holy Spirit softened Juvy's heart and he raised his head, saying, "I want to be a part of the family of God." We all prayed for him. He received the fullness of God and was married to Jesus that day. There was an immediate change in his life.

Juvy had life in his eyes, and he seemed so happy and excited about life. As we worked the next day, it was different than before. He was more passionate to work because he knew he was doing it for the Lord. As I watched the joy beam from his eyes, I thought of the years ahead for him. I thought about the decision that he made the night before and what new journeys he would take with Jesus.

JUVY'S EMERGENCY

The next morning, however, something happened. Just as the sun was rising over the mountains and we were starting our day's work, Juvy stumbled up to me, panting feverishly. He was out of breath and was holding his chest tightly. Something was severely wrong with him. All of our team members came over, concerned about Juvy's health.

After a discussion with Juvy's mother (who never took care of him), we discovered that there were multiple issues with his body that needed immediate care. The instrument makers and I decided to take him to the other side of the village to a nurse who helped people with minor sicknesses. As soon as the village nurse looked at him, she told us that we needed to rush him to the hospital.

With only a motorbike available, I was positioned on the back, holding Juvy tightly between me and the driver on the front. We drove Juvy to the closest hospital, which was nearly an hour away. We rushed him in, and the doctor examined him. Shaking his head in disappointment, the doctor explained that their hospital was not equipped to operate on him. They said that we would need to travel another eight hours to a German-led hospital. By that time, it was late afternoon and Juvy's body was not doing well. We jumped on public transportation in the city to get to the hospital as fast as we could.

When we arrived late at night, the German doctors assessed Juvy's body. They explained that what happened was he received a parasite from stepping in filthy water, and this parasite had traveled up his body and attacked his kidneys, heart, and brain. Unknown to us, he already had high blood pressure, dengue, brain cancer, and rabies before getting the parasite, but when the parasite attacked his body, some of these diseases, which had been lying dormant, flared up in his body, causing him to go into an emergency reaction. He was fighting for his life and was barely holding on. No one knew about all these problems—except Juvy. He just kept it in.

In the hospital bed, he lost feeling in his body and couldn't speak. He could only hear and see. I stared into his eyes, asking if he wanted Jesus to heal him and he raised one finger up, signaling to me that he agreed. I pleaded to God for his life because I didn't want him to go yet. I walked out into the frigid hospital hallway as I pleaded with the Lord about Juvy's life, saying that he needed to be healed. I had seen the Lord heal people so many times before, and I knew Juvy was also going to be healed. I prayed three times, confident that God would heal him.

But Juvy's body wasn't healed. We stayed with him through the whole night, praying fervently.

The next morning around 8:00 a.m., he passed.

A sense of sheer sorrow swept over our drained, feeble souls. We felt defeated. We arranged for Juvy's body to be taken back with us when we returned to the Manobo tribe. We slowly returned to the village with despair bending our shoulders because we tried our best and thought our prayers would heal him, but they didn't.

THE LEGACY OF A "NOBODY"

When we arrived in the village, his body was set in the center of town, and everyone gathered around to mourn. Many people came. Many people wept. I had never seen such mournful wailing like that before.

I was surprised to watch as many tribesmen came to grieve together. It was my understanding that Juvy was considered a nobody, but that wasn't the case. He was clearly a somebody!

During the funeral service that evening, Palu told the testimony of Juvy giving his life to Jesus, which had happened just two days before. People were amazed at this story of how God was so intentional in calling out to Juvy because He wanted him in His family. That's how much God cared for someone who was cared for by no other person in the world.

No one knew the full story of Juvy's life, other than that he was rejected by his father, that his mother was unable to properly nurture him, that he didn't have a proper home, and that he had major health issues. Nevertheless, Juvy was known for other things. He was the one who went from house to house, carrying a spirit of servanthood with him. He blessed people's fields for no wage except a bed to sleep in. He was the one who did the most horrible jobs in exchange for the least reasonable pay. He was fervent for life despite all of the wrong done to him. No one saw all the wrong done to him, except one—the Father—and the Father truly rewarded him.

Perhaps the reason why Juvy was a noble person despite all the wrong done to him was because he deeply desired a future that was better than what he had, and he knew he wouldn't obtain that joy by gaining earthly possessions. Perhaps he desired something deeper. That's the true heart that God searches for.

Many who sat around the funeral late that chilly evening came to realize the deposit that Juvy invested in the land. Many people were weeping, not necessarily because of Juvy's death, but because of God's love. God cared enough for Juvy that He saved him and gave him eternal life.

People were so moved by his story that his funeral became an altar. The breath of God came in the room, inviting many into His family. Twenty-eight individuals from that village gave their lives to Jesus that night. There wasn't even an altar call or someone preaching to them; Juvy's life and testimony was enough.

One boy's life was a testimony of God's eternal blessing to those who have the heart to say yes. Juvy's name lives on in that village because God honors the humble.

"Blessed are the poor in spirit, for theirs is the kingdom of heaven." (Matthew 5:3)

Humble yourselves, therefore, under the mighty hand of God that at the proper time he may exalt you, casting all your anxieties upon Him, because he cares for you. (1 Peter 5:6–7)

TEN
OBJA TRANSFORMATION

Our team of indigenous instrument makers were growing in the love of the Lord together. After we dedicated the instruments to worship the one and only true God, His blessing came upon the people and the sounds of worship they released. A heavenly overflow of God's presence, along with discipleship and the fellowship of believers, was so alive that there was no need to attempt to convert anyone. The light of Christ showed so radiantly in the midst of the troubled men and women that the culture of heaven was its own convicting source of evangelism. The people from outside just wanted in on what was happening.

The one thing that burned in our hearts beyond all this was the nearby unreached villages. There were still some remote villages in their tribe that had not yet had the opportunity to encounter Jesus. Of these, some heard about Jesus from a distance but had not heard directly, while others had never heard of Jesus at all. This, of course, just made me more thrilled to go there.

During that exciting time, we heard that a person killed

someone else in a distant village called Obja. Once this person was killed, the family members of the one who got killed had *pangayaw*, which means "the right to kill." It's similar to the English word *revenge* but is very different. Revenge means the right to get back at someone for what they did, but it stops there. While some might want to carry revenge all the way to the point of killing someone, we know we don't have that right. We don't get to take a life in revenge.

Among these people, however, pangayaw gives the right to kill—quite literally. If someone killed one of their family members, they had the right to kill. Even worse, it doesn't stop with killing the murderer. Pangayaw means they have the right to kill anyone, not just the person who killed their family member. In this way, this "right to kill" is a nasty cultural practice that can spread fast within many Manobo tribes. It starts with someone killing someone. The victim's family gains the right to pangayaw, meaning they have the right to take life just as life was taken from them. In anger, grief, and hatred, they kill anyone who they would like, often including innocent tribesmen, which then also gives their families the reward of killing. Though I don't understand the complete meaning of this cultural practice, I noticed that the recompense for pangayaw is death. It's eye or eye, tooth for tooth, death for death, and the story continues until many have the right to kill and many have died.

The only way to stop a pangayaw is that a large offering must be given, usually by the original killer. If the first killer will confess and make amends by offering a good-enough peace offering, the pangayaw will be settled and the families will drop the tension and move on. Though the offense doesn't ever seem to leave, there is a common understanding among the tribal culture that life has to continue on despite the grief of loss.

The news came to us that many people were being killed as the pangayaw continued to spread. This was all because the original killer never fessed up to his or her actions. Before long, many were killed—way too many. When the word got to us that there was pangayaw in this village, our hearts went out to them. After praying, we felt like the Lord wanted us to go to Obja. We didn't understand why; we just knew we needed to go.

RHYTHMS THAT BUILT RELATIONSHIPS

We started by packing many drums and musical instruments onto our motorbikes, which were the only type of vehicle that could make it into the remote villages. For getting to Obja, we could take motorbikes about halfway there, but then we had to hike the rest of the way. The motorbikes saved us at least a little from having to carry the drums so far. Then, as we departed from our village, many of the tribesmen prayed for us and sent us out. We knew the Holy Spirit was with us.

We sent a few people ahead of us the day before to scout out the land and inform the chiefs that we were arriving. This was part of the cultural protocol, to honor the tribe by letting them know we would be arriving. The village was not very far away, just about one hour of riding motorbikes up a tortuous path, then hiking another hour to the entrance of the village.

The hike was not too difficult. The only real challenge was crossing the rivers with large drums and backpacks on our shoulders. We made it, though, without losing anyone or damaging any of the delicate instruments.

All this made us happy, of course, but traveling there wasn't what we were concerned about. What concerned us was being there in the midst of the pangayaw. That's what we needed wisdom for.

When we arrived at the village, the chief welcomed us into

his home. Everyone had smiles on their faces as we settled into the small bamboo hut that we were staying in. The chieftain, called the *datu*, seemed happy upon our arrival, but very cautious as well. Thankfully, because of Palu and the instrument makers, we were able to communicate clearly that we weren't there with an agenda; we just wanted to be with them and bless them. Ultimately, we wanted the Holy Spirit to do what He does best, bringing His light and love, but we knew that their hearts had to be ready to receive. Only God can do that, so we decided that our approach would be simple: just hang out and connect with them.

Obja was spectacular. It was a serene mountaintop community that overlooked the Bukidnon mountain range of central Mindanao. A set of bamboo huts was placed neatly along the perimeter of the village and enveloped the community hall and play area for the kids.

Many undressed children stood on the outside of our hut, studying us in curiosity. I guessed they had never seen a White man before. In fact, all of the people of Obja stared at us to the point that we could feel our nervousness in our muscles. Each of us—guests and hosts—wondered what the other would do.

With all the hype of our arrival, the atmosphere was tense. What finally broke this tension was that one of our team members placed one of the drums on the ground and began to play.

The heartbeat of the tribe awoke as drums began to sound. No words were needed, just the collective rhythms of people playing and dancing. The children, who were a bit nervous at first, relaxed as they heard the sound of the Manobo rhythms and melodies for the first time. The adults all peeked out their heads from their huts to see what the sound was. In only a few minutes, we had the whole village in front of us, spectating, dancing, singing, laughing, and wanting to be a part of the sound.

The drums just kept going on, for days in fact, not because we planned for them to go on, but because the tribe just loved the sound. They wanted to be a part of it, like it was awakening something inside of them deeper than words could explain. At times, the kids would take the instruments and play, and at other times the adults would. In the midst of it, we would stop to talk with the locals about various things like farming and the current situation with the pangayaw. We didn't push an agenda on them. We simply let the Lord do the work as He wanted to do it.

LOVE, COMMUNITY, AND UNRAVELING MYSTERY

Every night, after our full days of playing and connecting with the locals, the datus would come visit us at the hut where we were staying. We would all sit around a large circle inside the hut with candles placed in the middle, lighting up the room dimly. The chiefs asked us many questions and vice versa. The conversation rolled on through the days we stayed with them, mostly revolving around the pangayaw topic.

The question everyone kept asking was, "Who started the pangayaw?" Someone initiated it by killing someone else's family member, but no one knew who it was. If they knew, the one responsible for starting the pangayaw would need to offer a large peace offering, such as valuable livestock for farming, in addition to a sacrificed animal, on behalf of the many lives that were already killed. The blood of the animal would give closure to the many families that were involved. As we dove deeper into the complicated issues revolving around the pangayaw, continuing into the wee hours of the night, we could not get away from the question of who started the pangayaw.

Night after night, we had deep discussions about the ongoing issues of Obja. All of us wanted to preach to them, but we didn't feel like it was time. If the gospel, being Jesus, was truly visible through us, then He would come to them at the right time. We felt like the conversation was deepening and their hearts were opening to Him more and more, but the time we could give to them was drawing short. It was nearly time for us to leave.

At hearing knocking on our wooden door on the last night before departing, we quickly stirred ourselves from our slumber and opened the door. What we saw made us smile. The datus had come to our hut again just as we were ready to sleep. As we quickly wiped the weariness off our baggy-eyed faces, they started asking us serious questions. The conversation quickly became real.

One datu asked us, "What is it that you have?"

We didn't completely understand the question, so there was silence in the room.

"What is it that you carry? Because whatever that is, that is what we want."

After he phrased it like that, we knew exactly what he was referring to. The datus saw the joy, love, and peace that we carried. We could hear it in their voices, that they wanted what we carried, or rather, who we carried.

We explained to him that it wasn't some*thing* that we carried, it was some*one*, and His name is Jesus. We explained that Jesus saved us from our fears, failures, and anger. He is the Son of the only true God who came to this world to live as we live and die as we die. But because He is God, He didn't have to die. It was His choice to die, because He knew that there had to be a perfect sacrifice given to save mankind from the worldwide pangayaw of sin and death. We explained that if anyone believes in Jesus and confesses that He is truly the God of all gods, He will come and save that person. God will give them a new life through the blood of the perfect Son, the ultimate sacrifice. Then Jesus will live inside the person, empowering and releasing all wisdom through His Spirit. The life of that person will be justified through the Father's love.

We all sat there in silence as it sank in. I wondered if our words meant anything to them. Did we speak too soon? Were they ready to receive this good news?

The silence continued until the datus spoke up, simply saying, "Thank you for coming to spend time with us." Then they all stood up and proceeded out the door.

We were unsure what happened. We were physically, spiritually, mentally, and emotionally exhausted by the end of that conversation. I still remember today how it felt, the feeling of lying down on the hard, wooden floor and adjusting my body to the most comfortable position possible as my heart cried out, "Holy Spirit, breathe on the words we spoke and let it catch fire in their hearts!" Within seconds, I was asleep.

A BEAUTIFUL CLIMAX

It seemed like I hadn't slept for five minutes when we were all awoken by knocking on the door. Arising from our deep stupor, we quickly dressed ourselves, realizing that it was already sunrise. We hurried to arrange the hut for hosting whoever was knocking on the door.

It was one of the datus. Opening the door slowly, we asked politely what he needed. "We would like to talk with you all," he said, and we scrambled to get our things situated.

We stepped out of the door and noticed that all the tribal datus were standing together in the distance. The datu who woke us was enthusiastic and began explaining to me what happened early that morning.

"After our discussion last night, we chieftains decided to get up early to talk before the sun rose. There was such a burning in our hearts after our discussion with you last night that we needed to talk. After thinking and talking together, we have decided that we want to follow Jesus Christ. We all decided that we want to be part of His family, and we desire that our whole village knows Him too. As we were discussing this, however, one of the datus told us that as much as he wants to give his life to Jesus, he knows that he can't do it until he tells the truth."

We all looked at each other, then one of us asked, "What is it that he needs to tell?"

Would you believe it? He confessed that he was the one who started the pangayaw!

We all stood, shocked. We looked over the datu's shoulder at the group of datus in the near distance, knowing now that one of them was the original killer who started the pangayaw. We could see which man it was. He stood near another datu, the one who's brother he had killed.

Why were these two men not trying to kill each other? Why was one not chasing the other? Clearly, the Holy Spirit was active in these people's hearts. What astounded me most was that they were the ones who decided to receive Jesus. It hadn't come from a preacher or an evangelist with an altar call, but it was the Holy Spirit who convicted the lying, killer datu that he needed to confess his sins and be forgiven.

They proceeded to explain to us that they weren't exactly sure what to do from there. They asked us to help them find counsel and pray together. We all gathered together to pray. Every single one of the chieftains drew together and forgave each other. It was a powerful time of forgiveness. They received the love of God into their hearts and felt the manifest presence of God. What a wonderful day for the kingdom!

This was a beautiful climax to our time in Obja, but we still needed to return to our own village that day. As we departed with backpacks and drums strapped to us, we told everyone,

"We will be back." The villagers all cheered with joy as they waved goodbye to us.

GOD'S KINGDOM KEEPS GROWING

We knew that this wasn't over yet. Now they needed to be discipled and taught how to grow in the Lord, but we walked away from Obja that day with great joy, knowing that God would continue to do what He started in them.

Sure enough, the Holy Spirit continued to grow His family in Obja. Hundreds of people gave their lives to Jesus. In fact, nearly the whole village of a thousand people began following Jesus. A church community was birthed, and from there they were all growing. We eventually supported one of our indigenous team members to help pastor their community.

We returned week after week to check on them and noticed that the Lord was blessing their land. Sure enough, it was raining only on their village, and the farmers were given wisdom from the Holy Spirit on how to grow their crops. The neighboring villages came to them, asking, "What is it that you have? Because whatever it is, that's what we want too." In this way, the gospel continued to grow beyond their village to areas that were even more remote.

This also led to bringing education to the village. The parents of the village were originally against educating the children because they thought that education would bring too many foreign things to their village. They feared that the children would learn, grow, and then leave the village.

Thanks to Palu and other Spirit-filled teachers in the area, however, the tribe was informed of the reality that the modern world is going to press in on them no matter what. Electricity will eventually come. Internet will eventually come. Foreigners seeking valuable minerals will eventually come. If they continue to stay uneducated, they will be unable to withstand the pressure of the modern world when it comes, causing them to be exploited—or even worse, dissipated and wiped out as a recognized people group. If they educate their younger generation, however, it will only strengthen them by giving them the ability to read, write, and formulate a true written language. They will be able to communicate clearly to the government concerning land rights and government partnerships with the indigenous people.

After much discussion and prayer, the elders accepted the invitation for the young children to be educated under the stewardship of Palu and the other teachers. A school was built under the canopy of the Department of Education, and the little children were able to learn for the first time in their history! They soaked it in like a sponge. As I write this book, we have already seen many graduates come through the school and go on to university in the city. Many of the students have returned to the village to bless and increase the land. Families are strengthened. Farmers have increased their produce and profits. And ultimately, the body of Christ has grown tremendously. To God be the glory!

The church that was birthed out of this season continued to grow by focusing on the education of the children. Many of the young students went through our education scholarship program that we created for students to get high school and college education. We saw many become professionals. This means a lot in their culture since many outsiders considered them low in the social and educational realm of society, but they aren't. They proved themselves capable through the power of the Holy Spirit living in them.

One of our rules we developed with the educational scholarships requires each student to give back to the community in some capacity once they become self-sustaining professionals. This became a key factor of stability for our education ministry because many of the students who were becoming professionals were hired by the Department of Education to return to their own village and establish primary schools. This continued to be a blessing in many people's lives. These poor tribal kids not only became professional teachers, but they were also discipled and Spirit-filled believers of Jesus Christ.

ELEVEN
KIRIBATI BLESSING

Though I had the urge to live with the Manobo tribe for the rest of my life and continue investing in them, I knew it wasn't the right thing. Perhaps some missionaries feel the need to invest their entire lives into a particular tribe, but I didn't think that was necessary for the work I was called to.

Christian missionaries in the first century, such as the apostle Paul, took initial trips to preach the gospel, find a man of peace, and establish a work of transformation in people's lives, and then they moved on to new places. In this, they always kept in touch with and visited the various churches they had planted as often as they could. They would often also send others to stay in the area, such as Paul sending Timothy to Ephesus, trying to help the new followers of Christ stay on the right path.

Knowing it was my time to move on, I said my sorrowful "see you later" to the Manobo tribe. As I left the Philippines, I knew that I would stay connected with the tribe. I didn't intend for my time with them to be over, but rather to step into a new dimension of ministry with them where the indigenous leaders took up the mantle of ministry while I kept in contact with them to help steward and nurture the work of the Lord.

> To Timothy, my true child in the faith: Grace, mercy, and peace from God the Father and Christ Jesus our Lord. As I urged you when I was going to Macedonia, remain at Ephesus so that you may charge certain persons not to teach any different doctrine, nor to devote themselves to myths and endless genealogies, which promote speculations rather than the stewardship from God that is by faith. The aim of our charge is love that issues from a pure heart and a good conscience and a sincere faith. (1 Timothy 1:2–5)

What was next for me? There was no doubt in my mind that the Holy Spirit was calling me back to Kiribati. I didn't have to think twice about it. I could feel and hear the nation calling me in my spirit man. I knew there was more that the Lord wanted to unlock among that people group; I just didn't know what it was. That was the faith journey I was on. I could feel the Lord's burden and heart for the nation, but I didn't know why. The faith action was to respond. I knew that if I didn't respond, I and the nation would perhaps be missing out on something. If I fell on my face trying, at least I could say I tried.

MY SECRET SOURCE OF FUNDING

You may be asking, "Where did you get all the money to travel around the world like that?" Well, I'll tell you. This is the best kept secret. If you understand this one secret, it will unlock prosperity and allow you to do what God has called you to do. This one secret has been tested and proven throughout time. If you understand and apply this one principle, you will, with no doubt, get what you need. Do you want to know what this secret is? Ready or not, the secret is . . .

Work.

Yes, you read that right. I worked. And I worked hard. Before I could go on any of these trips, I had to travel back to America and get back on my knees to install tile and hardwood. It was always hard work. Thankfully, because I learned how to install floors as a teenager, I was able to start a small floor-installation business to earn funds for all my trips. Each time I returned to America, I had a list of jobs to do. I would work from early in the morning until evening day in and day out.

Also, I would stay for free in my parents' basement. My dad used to say, "There are two ways to make money—by talking or by working with your hands. You have to choose how you'd like, and God will bless it."

> For you remember, brothers, our labor and toil: we worked night and day, that we might not be a burden to any of you, while we proclaimed to you the gospel of God. (1 Thessalonians 2:9)

I never felt the need to raise money by drumming up support. I felt like I needed to do my part in supporting myself. The other side of the coin of raising funds for missions, however, is donations, because people did catch the vision that God gave me for missions without me even asking and they simply wanted to give toward it. With much gratitude, I received those donations and was able to direct them toward my missions efforts.

JOINING GOD'S MOVEMENT IN KIRIBATI

After a few months of earning my wages for fare, I made my way back to Kiribati, taking Joel with me again. Though I knew

I didn't have enough money to live there long-term, I knew that what I had would at least get me there. The rest was up to God. It has been proven that when God calls, He supplies.

As the plane rumbled through the thick storm clouds, I leaned forward in my seat to gain some stability in my equilibrium. The pilot announced that it would be only an hour until we arrived on Tarawa island, giving immense relief to Joel and me. Soon after, our mid-sized jet descended through the thick Pacific storm, unveiling the open blue ocean below us with a small tropical island resting on top.

The first time we were here, we knew no one, but this time as we arrived, we were greeted by many Kiribati men and women. I knew the Kiribati language nearly fluently now. A fiery joy welled up inside me, knowing that this season of ministry would be a blessing to the islands of Kiribati. We reconnected with Katuba and the church that he was pastoring. They were eager for the Lord and wanted to go deeper in Him. I knew their community would be good soil where we could plant seeds of the kingdom.

As before, we didn't bring enough money with us to care for our needs. We lived day to day. Many days we didn't have money for the day, but God always supplied what we needed. One morning I woke up and I knew that I needed to travel to a certain village to meet with a pastor. It cost forty cents to get there and forty cents to get back, so I needed eighty cents. I looked in my wallet and pockets and saw that I didn't have any money. As small as this need was, I wasn't sure how I was going to get the money to go to that particular village to minister that day.

I proceeded to do my morning jobs for the Kiribati family who I lived with. My job was to collect the coconut sap by shimmying up four coconut trees with a sharp knife and bottles in my hands. While I stood at the top of the tree shaving the coconut sapling, I heard coins fall in my pocket. Stopping what

I was doing and placing the knife and bottles on a tree branch, I reached into my pocket to see what had fallen in there. Sure enough, there were coins! I pulled out all the coins and counted them. It was ninety Australian cents, the currency used in the Kiribati islands. I was amazed and perplexed by this. It was just enough money for me to get to and from the location I needed that day, plus ten cents.

After finishing my work with the family, I traveled on the public transportation to see the pastor who I needed to speak with. Upon arriving, I told him about the money falling into my pocket and gave him ten cents as a tithe to the church. It seemed like a joke, but it wasn't. It was a sincere gift, and besides, God has a great sense of humor. We laughed and proceeded to discuss what we needed to talk about.

Nearly every morning, the young people would gather together to pray and seek God's face. Joel and I would wake up at 4:00 a.m. to see the boys and girls already on their knees, praying and calling out to God. The power of the Holy Spirit would come on us all as we prayed for the nation. Many were healed and many were set free. We continued to fellowship, break bread together, worship, and teach under the large, thatched roof called the mwanieba. There was love and power in the fellowship with one another. It grew more and more as we invested our hearts and time into the land. It certainly wasn't accomplished by our great deeds and skills. It was purely the overflow of what happens when believers come together in unity and love. I was thankful to see this.

ON THE SHIP FOR AN ADVENTURE

Joel and I felt a pull to go to the outer islands. We were not sure exactly why, except that we knew there were people living in the outer islands who needed to hear the Good News. I knew that they already heard the gospel of Jesus Christ, but I could feel the Father's heart for them. We knew that the Father wanted them to truly encounter His love. We knew that His love would transform them. That's what motivated us to go to the outer islands.

After asking around, we found out that there was a small cargo ship called *Super Carrier* that was about to depart from Tarawa island to go south through the islands of Kiribati. We quickly packed our bags, not knowing what to bring since we didn't know how long we were going to be there. It was difficult to know what to pack. We grabbed a few bags of chips and some bottles of water and went to the port to find the ship.

Everyone was bustling around, loading cargo to the brim of the ship. The captain of the ship allowed us to get on, but I could tell that this wasn't going to be a relaxing vacation cruise through the tropical islands of the Pacific. This was a cargo ship, and in the captain's eyes we were also considered cargo. This reality hit me smack-hard when I looked into the depths of the wide-open ocean, knowing that once we embarked, we wouldn't be able to turn around.

We boarded the ship with lots of Kiribati people surrounding us. It was packed, but we found a small cabin with a bunk. Thankful to not have to sleep on a shipping crate, we squeezed ourselves into the bunk room and placed down our bags. It was dirty, and miniature roaches scurried around the beds and floor. The ship's large motor revved up as we glanced out of the small porthole, splashing water up to where we could see the spray.

It was exciting! We couldn't believe that we were actually doing this—riding a small cargo ship across the Pacific Islands. This was the beginning of an adventure!

The ship jolted as it disconnected itself from the wharf's dock. Almost immediately as we departed, an overwhelming punch of unease came over our bodies—sea sickness. The waves of the ocean continually jerked the small ship back and forth, knocking us around the room. Would we be dealing with this for the remaining five days on the ship? We could only wait and find out. But we had confidence. We were willing to face this continual pain in order to preach the gospel. Whatever it took, we were willing, as long as the kingdom expanded and Jesus's name was glorified.

MORE ADVENTURE THAN WE BARGAINED FOR

The porthole in our bunkroom had a small opening where we could get some fresh air. Joel and I both got as close as we could to it because we were lacking good quality oxygen. We were lightheaded and dizzy. This continued on and on.

Before too long, Joel, feeling extremely nauseated, jumped up and attempted to vomit out the porthole. Being dizzy, he missed the porthole and it hit me instead. The room was now covered in filth, which triggered me to vomit, and before we knew it, the whole room was even more filled with filth. This continued throughout the day and through the nights as well.

For the gospel, I kept reminding myself. We were tired and needed a solid ground to rest on, but we didn't get that for days. To make it worse, the affliction of the sea hit us full force. Sometime during that duration on the ship, Joel's ailment developed into an ear infection. He was disillusioned and couldn't see or walk straight. This frightened me, knowing that we were hundreds of miles in the middle of the Pacific Ocean without means of getting any medical help.

I left our bunkhouse in search of the captain. When I explained to him what was happening to Joel, he said he would be willing to examine him. Since we were very limited on resources, I thought the captain would be the closest to a doctor.

Joel stumbled into the captain's quarters. The captain, a

heavyset burly man with an untamed tongue, took a look at Joel's pitiful countenance. He examined Joel's eyes and ears, saying, "Hmmm." Then he looked at me with a disappointed expression and said in his burly voice, "He's got a bug in his ear."

I was taken aback. I thought, *He's got a bug in his ear?* "Those bleeping little roaches are attracted to the ear infection," the captain mumbled as if he'd seen it happen many times before.

Just hearing that made me want to go back to my bunkroom and hide, but I couldn't because I knew those roaches would be waiting for me there. The captain said he could take care of it as he turned and fumbled through his piles of random papers and objects on his table. Then he pulled out a straw that he must have previously used in a drink.

"Hold on there, son," he said, and he placed the straw in Joel's ear and attempted to blow out the miniature roach. I squinted my eyes in unbelief. Joel was leaning over awkwardly while the captain tried to blow it out. I was hoping the ship wouldn't crash while the captain struggled to excavate the roach, and while we didn't crash, that roach didn't get out. It was stuck.

We stumbled back to our bunkroom, discouraged and left with no option but to endure the smell, roaches, and seasickness for the remaining days of travel.

What felt like an eternity later, we looked out the porthole and could see something in the distance. It was a small, raised land—Tabetuea island! Finally, we had reached our destination.

The ship slowly approached the island, trying to avoid the coral reef wall. Since it was low tide, however, the captain was forced to anchor the ship far away from the island. This meant we had to walk with bare feet about a quarter of a mile on sharp coral to get to the island. We hopped in the water, then about waist deep, and waded through the sharp coral reef that was teeming with fish as our eyes looked toward the land.

To be honest, we felt pretty intimidated. Joel was still not feeling well at all. He was so disillusioned that I had to assist him in walking through the sharp coral reef. We looked at the coastline of the island and about one hundred people stood, waiting for the cargo and people to arrive. When we finally stumbled onto the island, all the people gaped at us because we were the only foreigners. And we were obviously not doing well. No one seemed to want to help, though. Here we were, missionaries to this foreign land, but we were the ones who needed help. Our mission to this island turned into a mission for survival. Everyone turned and walked away from us after getting their possessions.

THE PRICE OF VALUABLE LESSONS

Resting on the sandy beach brought comfort to our bodies, and we were relieved that we would not be tossed around anymore, but watching the captain and his ship embark to another island made me realize that we must face a new challenge. Where were we going to go on this island? I noticed one Kiribati man who seemed friendly. Gaining my confidence, I walked up with a smile, internally collecting my words to say in the Kiribati language.

"Hello! We are looking for a—"

Interrupting me mid-sentence, he said with a welcoming smile on his face, "Would you like a place to stay? You, please, come to my house."

Thrilled, we accepted his invitation and proceeded down the road to his village. Tabetuea was a beautiful coral island. This island was much more rural, and quieter compared to Tarawa island. There was not much electricity and only a few cars. Most people walked or rode bikes down the sandy path lined with coconut and pandanus trees. We came up to the man's home and met all of his family, who all had big smiles on their faces, just like the man had. They welcomed us, noticing that Joel was looking ill, and immediately assisted him, and with much more care than the burly captain.

I laid down that night in much pain from the long travel. I knew the Lord was going to turn this torturous trip into something beautiful. I could feel it, and I knew in my heart that there was a promise for this island.

At the same time, my body was tired and my mind was confused and discouraged. The trip was not turning out the way I thought it was going to. I had this vision that as soon as we arrived on the island, hundreds of people would turn their hearts to Jesus and revival would break out. But instead, we both lay there in intense pain.

The next morning, we woke up and Joel was still not feeling well. He needed real medical help. While it was deeply disappointing to me, I knew that we needed to go back to Tarawa as soon as possible. Our new hosts helped us find a radio to call the main island. We were able to secure an airplane flight back to Tarawa island. When the airplane arrived and we started climbing up its metal steps, I turned and looked at the island. With a deep yearning in my heart, I cried out to God, "Holy Spirit, come to this island!"

We arrived on Tarawa island, but we were not able to find the help Joel needed. This meant that he needed to get back to the United States as soon as he could. We collected all of Joel's belongings and took him to the airport. After some time, I was relieved to get an email from Joel saying that when he arrived back in the United States, he was immediately taken care of at a hospital.

As I reflected on all this, I learned some valuable lessons from our excursion to Tabetuea. First of all, if you can, go with locals. We knew this already, but we jumped ahead of ourselves when we heard of the opportunity that came from the ship that arrived at the port. If we had taken a local with us, things would have been much smoother. But despite how badly the mission went, it was not a failure because God saw our faith, aspiration, and passion for His kingdom. Even though we didn't see any immediate fruit, we planted our physical feet on the island in sheer faith, and we planted seeds of kingdom harvest in the spiritual realm. I knew the Lord would finish what He started on that island. As Scripture says, "And without faith it is impossible to please him, for whoever would draw near to God must believe that he exists and that he rewards those who seek him" (Hebrews 11:6).

MISSION EXPOSURE TRIPS

From that time on, I started traveling to new villages and other islands to preach the gospel with power and love, but now I went with the locals. There was so much more grace when I traveled with locals. They knew where to go and how to get there properly. They knew the cultural protocol that I was still learning.

I learned so much from the locals. I learned the language. I learned their culture. I learned to love what they love. I learned to laugh like them and enjoy the simple things in life. I even learned how to spear fish, although I was more likely to get speared than the fish. At least I still tried.

After some time learning these lessons, and with a greenlight from the Lord and the locals, I started inviting my friends from the United States to come on short-term missions to Kiribati. Since I knew I would be staying there for a long time, I thought that bringing people from the States would be beneficial in encouraging the Kiribati people in their faith. We called this endeavor Missions Exposure Trips, which gave people from the States a short-term exposure to the nations while also serving the long-term mission of what God was doing in Kiribati. It also gave the Kiribati people an opportunity to be encouraged by someone from outside their usual culture or experience. It was a glorious kingdom exchange.

One particular Mission Exposure team came for a week to minister on Tarawa island. We invited people from all over Tarawa and the outer islands to meet them. Hundreds and hundreds of people came, including—to my joy—a group of people from Tabetuea island, the island I had been forced to leave to get Joel the medical treatment he needed. This group who came from Tabetuea was extremely hungry for the Lord.

A powerful wind of the Holy Spirit blew through the main island where we gathered, and the Father's love filled hundreds of people each day. Many people were healed. We were absolutely astonished by God's divine power coming to touch these people He loved.

NEW LEVELS OF REVIVAL

One particular day, we were having a formal meeting, and many of the government leaders were present. The Speaker of the House of Parliament and his wife were seated in the front row. In the middle of the service, God's power started stirring in the room. The Speaker's wife had a very bad hip that needed to be replaced. She was scheduled to fly to Fiji to get a hip replacement, but God decided to heal it on the spot. She was healed instantly. As she shared about her healing, an eruption of glorious worship filled the large thatched-roofed meeting hall.

After her joyous speech, her husband, the Speaker of the House of Parliament, started sharing. As he stood up, the room became more sober in respect for who he was. He was tall, and a man of much authority.

After clearing his throat, he said, "About a year ago, I heard about Caleb and the ministry that he was doing on the island. I didn't like the sound of it, and I wanted to kick him out of the country. I just didn't understand what he was doing. But now I see the love and goodness of God. Praise God for all that He has done! Praise God for His love for our people here on this little island in the Pacific."

Turning to me, he apologized for trying to get me kicked out of the country. For me, it was a very sober moment because I had struggled with authorities for months while changing my Kiribati visa, trying to deal with issues that would otherwise force me out of the country. Standing there, with tears in my eyes and seeing the Speaker of the House with his newly restored wife, made me realize how God truly goes before us and fights our fights.

After our gathering was done, the ministry of the Holy Spirit continued to grow throughout the islands. We heard a report that Tabetuea started a new church fellowship on their island. The locals there started their own church fellowship under the canopy of Katuba's church. Hearts of men, women, and children grew deeper in the Lord. There was a shaking of the religious spirit as people yearned for a deeper truth of relationship with Him.

As the body of Christ continued to be strengthened, I kept inquiring of the Lord, "How should I proceed from here?" What I continually heard from the Lord was, "You are an inspiration to spur them on in their calling."

At that point in the trajectory of kingdom growth in Kiribati, we could have started our own ministry in the Kiribati islands, but I knew that if I started it as a foreigner, the DNA of the church would always be ruled and reigned by foreigners. He wanted the locals to embrace their true relationship with God and run with it. I knew deep down in my heart that God wanted and needed indigenous nationals to rise up and steward the gospel in their own country. If I were to stay any longer, the people would have too much dependence on me. I knew I had to go, even though it was hard.

At times, the best way to love is to let go. I knew I had to release them into the hands of God in order to not control the growth of what He wanted to do there. The growth of one's personal relationship with God is a sacred entity that I dare not intrude on without permission from God. I knew in my heart that it was time to step out so God could work a strengthening of His people in the land. This strengthening always includes growing pains.

The ultimate goal of any missionary is to assist the Lord in starting a fire—not a spark, not a smoldering ember, but a fire. The second goal is to hand the stewardship over to locals who will continue to fan into flame the gift of God. Katuba and all the pastors were the ones to do this.

This gave me joy, even in the difficulty of leaving, because I was confident that God would continue to steward what He started in that beautiful season with the Kiribati people. As John the Baptist said, "'He must increase, but I must decrease'" (John 3:30).

TWELVE
GLADYS

During my first visit to the Philippines, I received an email from the secretary of my home church in North Carolina. She mentioned that there was a missionary couple serving in the Philippines who had been sent from our church many years ago. I thought that it would be a good opportunity to connect with them while I was there, so I reached out to them. Their names were John and Esther. After receiving my email, they invited me to visit them at their home. Excited for this new connection, I hopped on a bus and traveled eight hours to their place in Baguio, Philippines.

Arriving at their cozy cabin in the mountains, I was comforted to hear the southern slang of their North Carolinian voices. John and Esther had been missionaries in the Philippines for nearly thirty years and they were still just as on fire for the gospel as they were when they started. It also just happened to be that John was originally from my little hometown in North Carolina. He still had a country accent, even after being in the Philippines for so long. It was just like the old saying, "You can take the man out of the country, but you can't take the country out of the man."

John and Esther had three children they had adopted from the Philippines. They adopted Gladys, their oldest, when she was thirteen, after her mother tragically passed away.

Their second child is Matthew, who was placed at the doorstep of the local pastor's home. Moved with compassion for the baby who was deathly sick, they brought Matthew home and cared for him. The doctors told them that he would die within a short period of time, but that wasn't the case. By God's grace and healing, the baby continued to live. Matthew is completely handicapped and unable to talk, but he can feel and see. He also has a big personality. John and Esther adopted Matthew and have cared for him since that time. There's much more to this part of their story, and it has been an incredible testimony of God's goodness in the midst of rejection and tragedy.

John and Esther's third child is Anna. She, too, was warmly welcomed into their home. I was impressed by the creativity and imagination of little Anna when I spent time with her. She was always setting up props in the living room to create an imaginary far-away scene. I could tell she would be innovative and artistic, and I could see that it was nurtured by John and Esther's intentionality and safe home.

All told, we quickly built a warm connection. My time with them was beautiful and refreshing, and I looked forward to more times with them in the future.

A few months later, I was traveling to Manila and had two days left before making my series of flights back home to North Carolina. As I entered Manila, I got a request from John to speak at their church, which was called Arise and Shine. This church was where John and Esther established their ministry, and it was a thriving community of believers.

THE MOMENT WE MET

The night before I left the country, I was standing in the courtyard of the pastor's home when we heard the entrance gate squeak open. A lovely young Filipina woman came through holding a bag of fish in her hands. She caught my eye because of her innocence and beauty. I was certainly not ever the type of guy that was caught by the beauty of women. One of the disciplines of Christians I had been taught is to have a self-controlled set of eyes. When this young woman walked by, though, I could see a purity in her that was unique. Before she passed us by, the pastor introduced her as Gladys, John and Esther's daughter. I was so happy to meet her since I had enjoyed my time with John and Esther so much at their home.

While Gladys kept holding the fish, we began some small talk about my missionary journey and her life as a nurse working at a local hospital. She also did lots of medical missions at that time, so we both had a similar desire to help the indigenous people of the Philippines. We talked for what seemed like three hours, but was really more like twenty minutes.

I learned that she was raised by her mother, while her father left after Gladys was born and never returned. Her mother, named Rosemary, worked hard to support Gladys and two other daughters, but they struggled. They were kicked out of their home at times and had to live under makeshift shelters. Rosemary wanted the best for her daughters, and through her hard work, she put Gladys in a Christian school, hoping to give her a better future. Not long after that though, unexpectedly and tragically, Gladys lost her mother from an asthma attack.

At that time, Gladys didn't have any place to go. Once the word got to the leadership of the Christian school that Gladys attended, they reached out to see how they might be able to help.

Well, those leaders were John and Esther. They opened their home freely to Gladys so she could have a good place to sleep. This was the start of a special relationship that developed between the three of them. Before too long, it was obvious that God led them to come together, not just to help Gladys in her need, but to form a family. I was nearly brought to tears thinking about how the Lord shepherded Gladys through the years.

Standing in the compound with the pastor, his family, and his friends, I could tell what they were thinking as they looked and giggled at Gladys and me standing beside each other and talking. Sure, Gladys was definitely delightful, but I wasn't interested in getting into a serious relationship. I had to focus on the course that the Holy Spirit had set out for me. I knew there was a time for certain things, and that was definitely not the time for a relationship, not with all I had to do in doing pioneering kingdom works in remote and sometimes dangerous villages.

THE WAY TO A MAN'S HEART

In those many years of living with tribal groups in the Philippines and Kiribati, however, I had to travel through Manila all the time. Since it is the capital city of the Philippines, I would have to fly in for one to two days on my way to the tribal areas of Mindanao or to the Kiribati islands. Each time I came through the area, John and Esther opened their home to me and allowed me to crash for a day or two. This always helped me because my travels were very long and tiring, and a break in the middle always helped. While there, I would often take the opportunity to speak to the students at their Christian school and encourage them in their walk with Christ.

On the last day of one of my short stays, Gladys stopped by to ask if I needed my clothes washed. I only had a handful of clothes, so I accepted her offer. Taking a basket, she placed my clothes in it and proceeded to her house to wash them. I knew this was an act of service because she had already worked long hours at the hospital and she needed rest.

I left to speak to the students for a few hours, and when I came back, I found the little white basket with all my clothes washed, ironed, and neatly folded. I was floored by her hospitality. Packing my suitcase, I began to take the clothes out of the white basket. After taking out the first few items, I heard a crackling sound underneath the clothes. There, sandwiched between the clothes and wrapped in foil, was a fresh batch of chocolate chip cookies. Gladys smuggled cookies in my clothes so no one else knew that she did it!

That was the coolest, sneakiest, and most romantic gesture anyone could have done for me at that time in my life. Remember that a pack of Swiss Rolls meant so much to me at that time that I fought a monster rat to protect them! I was a single, lonely missionary who didn't have enough money to even buy a pack of snacks at the store, so a home-cooked batch of cookies went straight to my heart. I know that she did it simply out of the goodness of her heart without any strings attached, but for me, I was marked. I was blown away by her act of kindness. That was the moment when things shifted for me, and I began to grow in love for her.

Stepping outside the pastor's home, I looked around to see if I could find Gladys and thank her, but she had already snuck away. I went back in and finished packing my bags with a deep longing in my heart for her.

Later that night I sat down with thoughts of her rushing through my head. As much as I longed for a potential relationship with her, I knew that the time was not yet. There was more that the Lord had for me to do before I could pursue anything like that. My assignment from the Lord was not complete and I knew it in my heart. Even though she seemed to be a beautiful person, perfectly suited for me, I had to remove myself from the emotion of it all. There was a faith journey that the Lord was inviting me on. I didn't know what the next steps looked like, but I knew it would be good—as long as my ears were attentive to His voice.

That day I made my way back to the United States, I said goodbye to all of my friends in the Philippines. I was heartsick, but through all of the emotion of leaving, I could feel the Father saying, *Do you trust me?*

THIRTEEN
THE WAIT

I was back in the United States for a short season to get some rest, as well as to work some tile and hardwood-floor jobs to earn enough funds for another journey. I was working to get back to the Kiribati islands, though, not the Philippines. At that time, I heard that John was making his way through North Carolina. When I heard this, my heart leaped inside of me with anticipation of a chance to talk to him. I thought this would be a great time to connect with John and share some of my heart about Gladys. Although I was nervous, I knew it would be the correct protocol if I wanted to approach Gladys about a deeper relationship.

John got to town, and we sat down for an afternoon coffee. As normal, we talked about our passion to reach the nations for God's kingdom. We talked about missions work and prayed together. It was like iron sharpening iron.

As our coffee cups were nearly drained, I stared at the table we were sitting at, attempting to collect the right words to bring up the subject of how I felt about Gladys. I didn't want him to think that I was building a relationship with their family to get Gladys. That was definitely not my plan, but I wanted him to know that I had feelings for her so that he would be aware. It would also give me clarity on how they might feel about Gladys and me building a relationship with each other. So many thoughts rushed through my head in those moments when my eyes were glued to looking at the table.

Just then, John spoke up and broke the silence. "Caleb, I don't mean to sound intrusive or anything, but have you thought about Gladys and you being together?"

Those words were like heaven breaking open to me! I could not believe it. My pensive face changed from intently gazing at the table to looking him in the eyes and saying, "Yes, I have."

I'll tell you, that changed the course of our conversation. I told him about my deep feelings for Gladys even though we had not spent much time together. I told him that I thought she was the one but that I had an assignment from the Lord to finish first in the Kiribati islands and tribal areas of the Philippines. The talk was long but needed. It gave both of us clarity on how to proceed and how to pray.

I felt relieved from all the wondering and unknowns I had carried through the previous months. The joy in my heart was so immense, I could have jumped out of my chair with joy, but I remained as calm as I could, even pretending to sip coffee from my empty disposable cup. We bowed our heads as John led a prayer to seal up everything we had discussed.

Leaving that conversation, I knew that it was completely in God's hands. If Gladys and I (who were on opposite sides of the world) were meant for each other, then God would lead us to be together. He would draw our hearts to each other like magnets.

JOY OF RELATIONSHIP, PAIN OF DISTANCE

From that day on, Gladys and I occasionally exchanged emails. She was very busy in the Philippines working in the hospital and helping with medical missions. Meanwhile, I was busy saving up to travel again.

After working on many flooring installation jobs, I earned enough money to make my way back to the Kiribati islands where I put my focus on the mission that God had laid out for me. This was the time when we started taking cargo ship rides to the distant islands of Kiribati to reach villages full of people who needed Jesus. It was a very fruitful time with many people coming to know Jesus, and we were planting new churches. We also started a small school of ministry to help the young believers become leaders in their community and villages.

All along as I did these things, my heart for Gladys never left me. She and I wrote letters to each other. Our letters took five to eight weeks to arrive, but they were always worth it. Our hearts grew closer and closer. I never knew what she felt because our letters were usually pretty shallow, but we did enjoy each other's encouragement.

Time went on and we stayed connected. I told Gladys that I would be returning to the Philippines in February and we would get to see each other. She said she was thrilled to hear that, which gave me a clue that she was interested in me.

The work in Kiribati was growing and expanding, which meant more things were demanding my attention there. The pastors of the churches were reaching out to me often. In some ways, this was wonderful because it was a measure of just how much God had done in the islands. The problem was that it was getting close to February and there was still more work to be done. I prayed and gave it to the Lord.

Just then the Holy Spirit spoke to me and said, *Your time here is not done yet. You need to stay in Kiribati and be focused.* This was hard for me to hear because my heart longed to be with Gladys. I knew that this would be hard for her to hear too. At that time, I decided to be real with her and explain how I felt. I knew I needed to send her an email and explain my true feelings toward her. I wanted it to be a better setting, such as being together on a moon-lit night or together just as the sun rose over the horizon, but it wasn't going to be together at all. In fact, the circumstance was just me in my hut late at night, typing on my beat-up laptop, trying my best to explain my heart to her. These were the words I wrote:

Dear Gladys,

I've been wanting to discuss the situation that both of us are in. Writing letters is not the best way to communicate, but this is all we have for now. I've been thinking a lot about our funny situation that we are in, and I've wondered what we need to do at this point. I guess you have definitely seen that I have feelings for you. We haven't spent much time together in real life, but after reading so many messages and letters from you and you reading so many from me, I feel close to you. You are a good friend and you've shown it by being faithful to message me so much!

I knew that at that point, our hearts would either separate or come closer—and it was the latter. Our hearts started to explode for each other. Being far apart and not being able to consistently communicate was hard. When I explained to her that my time in Kiribati needed to be extended, Gladys's heart sunk. I was also sad and embarrassed. I wondered if we could survive the wait.

Time went on and, while Gladys and I continued to write to each other, I stayed focused on the work of the Lord in the islands. We started hosting more teams of foreigners who wanted to get an experience of what God was doing in Kiribati. We continued our pastoral training and equipping. Days turned into weeks and weeks into months. And finally, I heard the Lord say as clear as day, *It is done.* I knew my assignment for the islands was finished. The pastors were trained, and islands were reached. There was definitely much more to be done, but I knew it wasn't for me to do. It was for the locals to do. I knew I would continue my work in Kiribati with a different approach, one that would be focused more on empowering the locals.

What that meant for me is that I could travel back to the Philippines—finally. I had another great conversation with John and Esther before the time came for me to return there. In the discussion, I told them that Gladys and I were starting to get serious about each other. I explained that I would like to dedicate a week to spending time with them and Gladys before I proceeded to the tribal areas of the Philippines to finish my work. John and Esther were thrilled to hear that.

REUNITED AT LAST

It was September when I left the Kiribati islands—seven months later than I had planned—and began the twenty-two-hour journey to the Philippines. John's family offered to pick me up from the airport in Manila. This would be the first time that Gladys and I would see each other in two years, but so much had happened in that time. Our hearts had grown close through all the letters, messages, and waiting.

I was on the edge of my seat emotionally as the plane landed. I hurried through many corridors, trying to find my way to her. When I stepped out of the Manila airport, a gust of hot, humid air met me, reminding me of the first time I stepped out of that airport years before. I looked longingly across the hundreds of people and bustling cars coming and going, and our eyes instantly met. It was her.

All my attention zoned in on Gladys as if all the people and vehicles disappeared. We both squeezed ourselves through the crowd, trying to make our way to each other. We finally embraced with a half hug.

A mix of emotions swept over both of us. My heart was

about to burst with God's pure love for her. But how did she really feel about me? How far should I go? Were we official? Was this really going to work for us to be together? We had not even spent any time together in real life, so touching each other even in something as simple as a hug felt both delightful and awkward at the same time. As much as I wanted to sweep her off her feet romantically, I knew that it would take time for us to learn to be together in real life.

Seeing John and Esther again was also a joy. We all jumped in their vehicle to travel back to their place. I rented a home down the road from their home for a week.

Obviously, Gladys knew I would be nearby during that week, but what she didn't know is that I had planned the whole week strategically as a week of dating and getting to know each other. Though I could go into detail about all the fun things we did, I will spare you. Needless to say, we both had the greatest week we had ever had. We went on walks, caught up on a thousand stories, traveled to touristy spots in the Philippines, and so on. Throughout the whole week, wherever we went, it seemed that Creation itself was joining us in worship together. I can't even express what this really meant, but I think my journal entry from that week explains it nicely:

> Gladys and I ventured out to Mount Makiling where we hiked through the botanical garden. It seemed as though all of nature was responding to us in harmony. All we could do was worship the Lord. I remember us stepping into the woods and all of the bugs began to make their loud ringing noise so it filled the whole forest.

Later that day I asked Gladys, "Do you like rainbows?"

She responded, "Yes, I love them, but I haven't seen one in a very long time."

Sure enough, later that week, as if God Himself painted it

across the whole skyscape, a rainbow stretched before us with another rainbow encircling it. Gladys and I stood in awe of God's bountiful blessing. To me, it was confirmation of our union. Our short time together was supernatural and opened the door to my love for Jesus even more. I know that sounds weird, but I walk in a greater level of worship because of the deposit He put in Gladys.

As much as I would have loved to kneel down and hand her a plastic ring at that moment, I knew the Lord needed me to finish the work we had started among the Manobo tribe. The spectacular week of dating was over, and it was time for me to depart. At the same time, though we had not discussed it yet, we knew marriage was around the corner.

LABOR TO FINISH WELL

Arriving again in the tribal area meant I would not hear from Gladys. There was no cell phone signal, and it was not easy to travel to the closest city. Incredibly, this village that was part of the same nation in which Gladys lived was more remote in some ways than even the tiny Kiribati islands in the very middle of the Pacific Ocean.

I returned my focus to the Lord's work. By this point in ministry, I had learned that ministry is like a snowball—once it starts rolling it will build, but if it stops rolling, it will get stagnant and melt over time. Since a lot of my work for the Lord was in establishing new ministry in new locations, I needed to learn the secret of passing the baton to locals who would carry on the work. This would keep the ball rolling so that the Lord's work would continue. The Holy Spirit started something so great in my previous days with the Manobo that I couldn't leave it, because then it would stagnate. I couldn't leave it and come back years later, just assuming everything would be the same. I needed to help them lay hold of God's promise from Scripture,

"And I am sure of this, that he who began a good work in you will bring it to completion at the day of Jesus Christ" (Philippians 1:6).

During these next few months, the local believers and I focused a lot of our energy on a new village called Obja. This is when the beginning stages of the Obja testimony started, where a whole village came to know Jesus. I'm thankful that the Father led me to be a part of that amazing transformation. We also developed a team of indigenous people who could carry out the ongoing work of the Lord in that region.

After a few months, I was ready. I felt the same words flow through my spirit that I had heard in Kiribati, *It is done*. I knew Gladys was waiting patiently for me. I discussed my arrangements with John about proposing to Gladys and then traveled to see her.

MADE FOR EACH OTHER

God gloriously arranged for me to propose to Gladys in her hometown. She had been born and raised there by her mother. It created another chapter in Gladys's beautiful story of redemption to invite her into a lifelong union of marriage in that same small town, located beautifully on the coast of the South China Sea. She said, "Yes!" so excitedly that it was as if she was really saying, "It's about time!"

It was a splendid season, with lots of excitement in the air. Gladys and I got married in the Philippines. My parents and a few friends of mine came from the United States to join all of Gladys's family and friends in celebrating the beautiful union.

After the official wedding, we were invited by the Manobo tribe to celebrate a tribal wedding. We were all dressed in tribal clothing and had a company of musicians and guards bring us to the center of the village where the ceremony of marriage was conducted. Before I could marry Gladys, I had to pass the test of stabbing a spear into a log with only one chance. By God's grace, I successfully stabbed the log, which meant I was "man" enough to marry Gladys. In this tribal wedding, nearly one thousand people from the tribe came to celebrate Gladys's and my union in marriage. This was not only a wedding between Gladys and me, but it was them adopting us into their tribe. We were deeply honored.

Our initial six months of marriage was marked with God's presence and peace as we took a sabbatical in order to truly get to know each other. Of course, we had a big learning curve and worked through lots of kinks, but the important thing is that we worked through them and didn't ignore them. This time of sabbatical gave us the freedom and time to learn about each other before God launched us into raising children and ministering hand-in-hand. Gladys and I still smile when we think about that time.

Not long after Gladys and I got married, we sat down and went through old photos and videos of each other. We reminisced about our beginning days of getting to know each other in the mission field. Looking through all the photos brought tears to our eyes, but there was one photo that shocked us when we saw it. This photo made us blink and rub our eyes to see if it was really real. It was the first picture we ever took of us together. In the pixelated photo, Gladys and I stood beside each other with nervous smiles as we posed for the photo. We looked like kids. The pastor's home was in the background. There was a dog back there too, and some laundry baskets where they handwashed their clothes—a typical scene you'd see in urban Philippine areas. But something stood out that we had not noticed before: Gladys's shirt. It was a blue shirt that you could tell had been worn many times in the past—not holey and scruffy like mine, just a well-used and well-kept shirt. The words printed on it in bold letters with a fancy font said, "When God made YOU, He must have been thinking of ME."

Yes, that was the first photo of us together that was taken. It was clear that God did, in fact, think of us when He made us. It reaffirmed in me that I needed a wife, and she needed a husband, and God pre-ordained us to be together. Though marriage is not for everyone, it was for her and me. We needed each other.

A NOTE FROM ESTHER

It was the spring of 1999, and John and I had been married for nearly seven years. We were very involved in helping out at the Christian academy in the Philippines where Gladys had been a student since third grade. Gladys stood out to us because of her sweet spirit.

Each year I would have each grade level of my girls' physical education class spend a night at our place. Gladys's mom said she would allow Gladys to spend the night if she could meet me first. We met outside a nearby theme park where we would sometimes take the students. I assured her that we would take good care of Gladys if she stayed at our house. Little did we know that would really mean for her future. It was only a month later that we received word of her mother's untimely passing.

We told the pastor of our church that we would be glad to welcome Gladys into our home if she needed a place to call home. Her grandmother lived too far from the school for her to travel there daily, so it was decided that she would move in with us. In April, shortly after summer break began, we went to pick up Gladys. When we got to where she was staying, we were expecting to load boxes of her belongings into our vehicle. To our surprise, she walked out with just one small box and a duffel bag, ready to start her new life in our home.

It was two years later that Matthew came to us with many needs, and Gladys didn't hesitate to jump right in and help us care for him. While on one of our many stays at the hospital, the nurses encouraged Gladys to apply for the nursing school that was connected to the hospital. She was just finishing up her senior year in high school at the young age of sixteen. Nursing was a perfect fit for Gladys with her sweet spirit and her servant's heart. It would be another ten years before Anna came on the scene with all her energy and pizzazz, but, as with Matthew, Gladys jumped right in, and her God-given mothering skills shined. Anna adored Gladys and still does today.

There was no doubt in our minds that Gladys would one day be an amazing mother and ministry partner for someone, and we are so happy to see this fulfilled with Caleb.

FOURTEEN
BATTLES

The neighbor's alarm clock (aka, rooster) stood on the roof of our home, attempting to wake the entire village, as was his custom. Waking up in the Philippines was always like waking up in a sauna, but this time it was extra hot and humid. I was normally already awake anyway, as I have always loved to wake up before the sun rises to meditate on God's mercies. As His Word says, "The steadfast love of the LORD never ceases; his mercies never come to an end; they are new every morning; great is your faithfulness" (Lamentations 3:22–23).

This particular morning, I needed new mercy from the Lord. I finished my intentional time with the Lord and began reading my emails. As I scrolled through them, I found one from one of our young leaders from Kiribati. I opened the email excitedly since I had not heard from this young leader for a long time. The message was short and shocking. As I read it, I sank into my seat.

It read, "Karebwa, aio te rongorongo. E mate ptr Katuba." (Caleb, this is the update. Katuba is dead.")

I didn't know what to think or how to even respond to such

a punch in the face. This was my best friend in Kiribati to whom I was planning to return soon. This was the man the Lord brought into my life, the man of peace and my co-partner in ministry in the islands of the Pacific. All of our ministry in Kiribati was held together by this one solid relationship. And now it was gone!

No one understood why or how Katuba died. He was only fifty years old and was healthy all the way up to his death, but he was gone, just like that. A deep sadness overwhelmed me. Gladys walked into the room, read the email, and placed her hands on my shoulders.

I knew I needed to get back to Kiribati to be with my Kiribati family and help comfort them, but how was I able to do that with all the other things I was stewarding? At that particular time, much of our attention was on the tribal ministry in the Philippines. The blow of hearing about the death of Katuba came at a time when I needed to focus on many other things.

Katuba's death, however, gave me great concern for the body of Christ in Kiribati. With him gone and me far away, I didn't know who would lead the movement God had begun there. My heart longed to know how they were doing. I knew that Katuba was the essential leader among the renewal that was happening across the Kiribati islands. Since I was Katuba's partner in ministry, I knew I needed to be there to secure the process of choosing the next generation of leadership and how that leadership should be structured.

THE FIRST SIGNS OF TROUBLE

After seeking the Lord and receiving much advice from my mentors, I decided to take a trip to Kiribati by myself while Gladys stayed home. My travel there was long and harsh. On the plane, I strategized in my mind about which particular places I would visit, who I would meet with, and what I would say to them.

I knew that the first place I should go was our main church. When I arrived there, I could meet with Katuba's family and all the other church leaders. I had my plan.

My Kiribati family picked me up from the airport and I made my way to their home for the night. Thankful for my pandanus tree-built hut, I laid down for a deep sleep on the lumpy branch surface with the gentle Pacific wind blowing upon my chilly body. Waking early the next morning, and after a wonderful time of sharing stories with my Kiribati family, I departed enthusiastically to get to Eita to see the church members.

I got on public transportation to go to Eita. Bopping up and down as we zoomed down the sandy road, I gazed out the window, seeing mothers selling fish and children running along the roadside. I got lost in the joy of seeing the Kiribati life again but was jolted suddenly by a Kiribati man's voice calling, "Karebwa! Karebwa!" (Caleb, Caleb).

I turned around and noticed that it was a man named Joshua, whom I knew from many years before. He was a pastor and a vital part of the renewal happening in the Kiribati islands. He said, "I'm so glad to see you here again! Where are you going?"

I replied, "I'm going to Eita to see Katuba's family."

Concern filled his face and he quickly replied, "You need to be careful."

Both shocked by and interested in his comment, I leaned in and asked, "Why should I be careful?"

Lowering his voice, he said, "There is a new leadership that has come to that church."

A deep lump developed in my throat as I asked him, "What happened? Who is it?"

"It's a different church from another country, and they don't believe the same thing we believe."

As our conversation got deeper, he told me everything that had unfolded during the previous months. He said that a foreign missionary had come to the island to attempt to start a church. This particular missionary wanted to plant a church in the islands to spread their belief among the Kiribati people. This belief system is in the form of Christianity, but very different from what the Kiribati believers already knew and lived. In short, there were major differences in this particular religion that were clearly not biblically accurate.

Much of my effort among tribal people had always been put into connecting different Christian churches together despite different opinions on biblical interpretations, but this particular belief was completely off. From my limited knowledge of the belief, I knew that it was a religion that was close to hitting the target yet managing to miss the bullseye completely. It was close enough to pull you in, but far enough to take you away from true fellowship with the Triune Godhead and the relationship that He provides. Many have been led astray by this theology, drawn to the effort of working for their salvation instead of receiving it through the finished work of Christ Jesus.

As Joshua explained more about how everything unfolded during the previous months, I was saddened and unsure about how to respond. He told me that the missionary who brought this religion had come to the church after Katuba's death. When he saw the opportunity, he told all of the community that his supporting church would grant them funds to grow their church buildings. He used prosperity teachings to woo them in. The missionary told them not to listen to me if I came back because he says I am a worshiper of many gods and I am taking them away from the true gospel. After many Bible studies, the missionary was able to convince some of the main leaders to follow him. After these leaders had turned, the whole church followed them into the same path of teaching.

SEEING IT FOR MYSELF

Still in total shock, I stared at Joshua in unbelief. Then shaking my head, I told him that I knew that I could still visit the families in Katuba's church because we were so very close. I had confidence also that all that I needed to do was have a clear and solid conversation with the leaders of the church and they would realize that the missionary's belief system was not quite on target. I knew that after our conversation, we would resolve the problems and learn how to move forward in love.

Despite Joshua's warnings, I decided I would make my way to Eita to see the church. Joshua followed me but stayed back some distance away. He wanted to be there for me just in case I needed help, but he didn't want to be noticed by the church members. He hid in the distance behind some coconut trees while I strolled quite confidently into the village to visit the church.

Arriving at the church, a flood of memories of the renewal, miracles, and the many times of glorious worship filled my mind. I stepped toward the large thatched-roof meeting hall, the mwanieba, where we had so many times of soaking in God's presence. As I approached the structure, one of the young children ran out in front of me and called out, "Karebwa!" with a playful, innocent expression. I embraced the boy and told him to go and tell the leaders to come meet me. I lowered my head as I stepped into the mwanieba, then took off my sandals.

After some time, one of the main leaders, his wife, and a few other leaders walked slowly into the meeting hall. I could tell they were thrilled to see me again but burdened by the death of Katuba and the transition they had faced. With an ashamed but stern composure on their faces, they said, "Karebwa, you are not welcome here anymore."

My heart sunk. I scrambled for words, not even knowing what to think in English, let alone in Kiribati. They shook their heads and said, "Why did it take you so long to get back?"

I looked determinedly down at the hard concrete floor, trying to gather my words together. "I have been waiting for the right time, and we have been very focused on the Lord's work in the Philippines. I didn't realize that you needed me here so quickly."

I knew my words were not the right ones; I just didn't know what to say. They continued, "We waited and waited for leadership to help us follow what God was going to do next after Katuba died, and since you didn't come for so long, we had to change our plans."

Those words struck me hard, and I didn't know how to properly respond in the moment. They apparently didn't care too much that the Lord had led me to help other indigenous tribes find the Lord or that I'd married the love of my life. They were too focused on their own problems, including a lack of leadership, to pick up the work on their own. I tried explaining the importance of continuing to steward what God started, but they didn't respond to me. I knew that I couldn't get anywhere with them because they already made their allegiance to the other missionary who promised them more money and fame. It was the poverty and entitlement spirit at its best, and I didn't want anything to do with it.

I knew I wasn't in the missionary competition business. I learned from an early age that I shouldn't get into the habit of fishing in other churches' ponds, but that I fish instead for people who are lost and broken, people who still need Jesus. In that moment, looking at their determined hearts, I turned my heart to God and offered them to Him.

I was sure in my heart that I knew what the real problem

was—they were sheep without a shepherd. Jesus is their True Shepherd, but Katuba was their community's shepherd who saw clearly the leading of the True Shepherd's voice and helped lead the corporate community in that direction. Every community needs some type of leader or team of leaders who are focused on the True Shepherd. Since Katuba was gone, other so-called shepherds came to lead them in a different direction.

PROCESSING WITH THE REMNANT

I left that meeting with great sorrow. It didn't have anything to do with the loss of numbers of people, fame, or material blessing; I was simply downhearted because people I deeply loved turned their backs on the Lord for money and material blessing. I was angry. I saw how the enemy had stolen the hearts of a community that was beginning to bring transformation to the nation. There was nothing else I could do.

As I stepped out of the mwanieba, Joshua met me, and we exited the compound. Holding back tears, I waved goodbye to all the cheery faced children as they ignorantly called out, "Tiabo moa, Karebwa" (See you later, Caleb).

There were, in fact, many leaders of the church who did not want to follow in the path of the new church theology. They felt a conviction in their heart about it and decided to walk away. This was a big ordeal and many of the key leaders left. The leaders and members who left had migrated to the church compound nearly thirty years before, residing with their fellow church members. This meant that when the church members left the church, they also had to pack all their belongings and move all they had to a new location.

Joshua and I traveled to visit them so we could give them some encouragement as they were making this new transition. As we all gathered under a small hut, we mourned the death of

Katuba and shared our hearts about the tragic change of the church community. It was a lot to process and deeply sorrowful to face in the midst of losing a prominent family member.

But despite all the sorrow, there was a thread of hope. We were hopeful because these leaders had the wisdom to move despite the pressure and temptation. We were confident that after the season of mourning, there would be a season of harvest again.

As we all prayed together, we chose to speak blessing over the church and the new missionary's endeavors. We sincerely called on the goodness of God for them in faith, knowing that He would continue to have His way in their hearts.

THE MOST IMPORTANT LESSON

My time in Kiribati was short, but God had bigger purposes in it than I understood at the time. Looking back now, I see that the Holy Spirit completely and perfectly arranged every step during my short time on Tarawa island. Meeting Joshua again was completely an arrangement from God. If I had not met him that day, many other things in the future would have never unfolded. Through Joshua, we began to reach many other islands and nations in the Pacific.

In the natural, though, it looked like everything was taken. It looked like all the work of the Lord was stolen and gone. In reality, however, it was far from that.

It's like a healthy tree that always gives fruit. If a healthy, fruit-bearing tree is chopped down and taken away in the natural, it seems like the tree is destroyed, but that is far from the truth. Before it was felled, that healthy tree dropped hundreds and thousands of fruits on the ground, and all that fruit had seeds in it. Those seeds wait in the ground, dormant until the right season. When the tree is taken away, it allows the sunlight to shine on the ground, causing the seeds to have just the right amount of soil, dirt, and sunlight. The seed that was once dormant will now begin to sprout because the sunlight it needed was introduced. In the spirit realm, God's Word is fulfilled that says, "I planted, Apollos watered, but God gave the growth. So neither he who plants nor he who waters is anything, but only God who gives the growth" (1 Corinthians 3:6–7).

I knew in my heart that even though this movement of the Holy Spirit was chopped down and taken away, like a large fruit-bearing tree, there were many seeds that were lodged in the hearts of hundreds of people in Kiribati, and no one could ever take that away. The joy is that God is the one to bring the increase, not me and not the other leaders. Only God can do that, at the right time and season.

In the following years, many situations like this would mark me—relationships torn from me, people turning from me, persecution, lies, and even threats to my family and closest friends. Through this revelation about who is responsible for seeds of the gospel, the Holy Spirit gave me help to hold on through all those difficulties. I also learned the value of holding my ground when things are not right. The important thing is to stay abiding in Christ, no matter what! The root, being Christ, is the lifeline and source. Without the root, I would have no good fruit in my life.

In the years following that event in Kiribati, I began to really understand the apostle Paul's words. I knew that at times I would be watering, while at other times I would be sowing seeds. The important thing that I learned is this profound statement: Jesus is the Builder of His Church. Many leaders in churches all over the world have to grasp the reality that Jesus is alive and active. As leaders, we need to stay in the lane God has given us and trust Him to do what He said He will do.

Concerning many of the battles we face, we have to come to the reality that God will ultimately win this war no matter what. Perhaps there are some moments when God allows the enemy to win a battle, but ultimately, God has already won the war. I have rested in this truth and hope, that Jesus did it all on the cross. He has won it, and His promises are sure.

> "And I tell you, you are Peter, and on this rock *I will build my church, and the gates of hell shall not prevail against it.*" (Matthew 16:18, emphasis added)

> When Jesus had received the sour wine, he said, "It is finished," and he bowed his head and gave up his spirit. (John 19:30)

FIFTEEN
MOVING FORWARD

At this pivotal juncture in our ministry to the unreached peoples of Southeast Asia and the Pacific Islands, we found ourselves actively engaged in twelve distinct locations. Our primary focus revolved around expanding the kingdom of God, and we achieved this by establishing diverse ministries such as feedings, medical missions, instrument-making, pastoral training, agricultural assistance, and educational scholarship programs. Remarkably, the Lord paved a path in all these where no human effort seemed possibly effective.

Amid our relentless efforts, we encountered substantial backlash and persecution from various angles. Nevertheless, we pressed forward with determination. It was during this time that we began to discern a fascinating pattern: persecution acted as fuel for the fire of God. We were astonished to observe that the more persecution we faced, the more the gospel spread! It was a fresh revelation of Romans 8:28, affirming that all things work together for good for those who love God and are called according to His purpose.

One particularly memorable event occurred when we

received an invitation to preach the gospel in a village comprised of around five hundred individuals. As Gladys and I, along with our indigenous missions team, arrived in a caravan of motorbikes, we were greeted by the entire village who had congregated at the central meeting place. It was clear that there was ample anticipation in their hearts to receive the Good News. We were informed, however, that a militant rebel group had encircled the village, harboring hostility toward our message. The village elders cautioned us that sharing the gospel with the entire village might instigate an outbreak of militant warfare. Although such situations had become familiar to us, we proceeded with caution.

After fervent prayer and with the peace of God, I felt compelled to preach the gospel boldly and without compromise. Indigenous leaders who accompanied us took the stage first, sharing their personal testimonies. I observed the profound connection forged between the locals and these leaders, which fostered an atmosphere of peace. Seizing the moment, I rose to preach the gospel, fearlessly proclaiming the saving and redemptive power of Jesus. As I preached, gunshots erupted from the outskirts of the village—the rebel group had opened fire. Unbeknownst to us, though, a defensive military force had been dispatched to shield us from their attacks. It was a division of the nation's defense force, divinely appointed to safeguard our mission. Unfazed by the continuing gunshots, I pressed on with unwavering boldness and the Lord moved powerfully in the hearts of the people. Many individuals embraced Jesus that day, marking a turning point for their village.

Once the dust settled and Gladys and I finally had a moment to reflect on that adventurous day of missions, we gleaned several insights that provided clarity for our future endeavors. The gospel was undoubtedly shared, and the rebels were unsuccessful because of God's divine grace and protection. It became evident that in the future, however, the Lord would grant us wisdom to preach the gospel effectively while avoiding situations like the one we encountered. We realized swiftly that the key to this lay in empowering the indigenous leaders.

We took note that the gunshots only rang out when I stepped forward to speak. As the only foreigner present, I unintentionally drew their ire. Perhaps if I had not been there, things might have unfolded more peacefully.

Yes, the truth remains that the gospel brings division. Scripture clearly shows that Christ Jesus is either a cornerstone or a stumbling block. Wherever Christ is preached, division is inevitable. This is stated in 1 Peter 2:6–8:

> For it stands in Scripture: "Behold, I am laying in Zion a stone, a cornerstone chosen and precious, and whoever believes in him will not be put to shame." So the honor is for you who believe, but for those who do not believe, "The stone that the builders rejected has become the cornerstone," and "A stone of stumbling, and a rock of offense." They stumble because they disobey the word, as they were destined to do.

In Matthew 10:34, Jesus Himself declares,

> "Do not think that I have come to bring peace to the earth. I have not come to bring peace, but a sword."

We made it abundantly clear that we would never be ashamed of the Good News of Jesus. Divine wisdom could, however, guide us away from falling into traps set by human agendas that seek to dismantle God's work. From that point forward, our prayer life underwent a transformation. One of our deepest supplications to the Lord was, "Send indigenous workers for the harvest!"

Little did we realize that God's true desire was exactly that—to raise up workers for the harvest. It was a "they must increase, and I must decrease" moment. The time had come for Jesus to manifest Himself through them among their own people.

As I delved into the book of Acts, I discovered profound insights. Just as Jesus commissioned His disciples for their apostolic journey to preach the gospel, they embarked with the power of the Holy Spirit. Further into Acts, we witnessed the way that many missionaries, including Paul and Barnabas, initiated the work of the Lord in foreign lands and swiftly appointed others to continue the mission.

Painful though it was, this experience underscored the need for an indigenous-led movement, rather than another foreign-led organization.

It often amuses us how we stumble upon the will of God. We might attribute the establishment of God's kingdom on earth to our strategic ideas, but the truth is far from that assumption. Jesus Himself builds His Church. It is as if the Holy Spirit gently nudges us in the right direction, keeping us on track, even when we are unaware, and that is precisely what happened to us. As we beheld the powerful indigenous men and women walking alongside us, we realized that we were meant to entrust everything to them. Yes, we were meant to give everything to them, and more.

The following stories serve as examples of how the indigenous people were empowered as we relinquished control, allowing the Holy Spirit to work through them and multiply the expansion of God's kingdom.

SIBAANAN VILLAGE

Sibaanan was a village comprised of refugees from the deep jungles who had been forced out of their original dwellings by a rebel army. These hunter-gatherers, who were accustomed to surviving off the jungle's resources, were now confined to a single area and faced starvation. This dire situation gave rise to tension and strife within the village as disputes over land rights and food resources escalated. Moreover, the absence of running water and electricity compounded their hardships. Upon learning about the plight of this village, we began to make frequent visits to provide agricultural assistance.

The village elders gradually expressed a desire to learn more about Jesus. After multiple two-to-three-day visits, we discerned that sending an indigenous individual to live among them would be the most effective course of action. This decision required a leap of faith from all parties involved.

At that time, a recent graduate from our scholarship program had obtained certification as a teacher through the Department of Education. This young tribal man, now a professional educator, was assigned to this broken and destitute village. He began teaching basic education to the young children beneath a large-canopied tree. He built favor quickly with the parents, who then requested instruction from him in the ways of Jesus.

Within six months, a church was established, and fellowship meetings were conducted daily in the teacher's home. People began to experience the goodness of God, which fostered unity within the village and led them to walk in the way of Jesus. As I write these words, that young man now has a family with multiple children. A school building has been constructed to provide education to the children, and believers are growing in the fullness of Christ. The village now has access to running water, electricity, and, most importantly, peace.

JOSHUA AND HIS ISLAND

In the islands of Kiribati, Joshua received a calling through a vivid dream to reach the remote islands of his nation. Joshua and his wife Tarawa obeyed God's directive, returning to Joshua's original home island, which was located a considerable distance from the main island. This particular island only welcomed its native inhabitants and rejected any foreigners, making Joshua's presence vital due to his heritage. Guided by the divine plans of God, Joshua ventured to the island. Initially, the people were reluctant to receive his message, but when the Holy Spirit descended upon them like fire, everything changed. Many of Joshua's family members, who had not seen him in over thirty years, were baptized in the Holy Spirit and experienced divine healing. This miraculous encounter ignited a spiritual awakening in the hearts of the people. To this day, Joshua and his wife continue to be a dynamic force for missions on this island.

ANSULAO AND CHRISTY

Another remarkable couple from our indigenous team, Ansulao and Christy, completed their studies and expressed a deep desire to serve the Lord in any capacity. Ansulao, who had always been my right-hand man, dedicated himself wholeheartedly to the Lord's work.

Shortly after his wife gave birth to their first child, they were asked to lead a dwindling church in a distant location. When they arrived and assessed the church's condition, they recognized the urgent need for revival. The church, now thirty years old, had dwindled to two quarreling families. Though the task ahead seemed daunting, Ansulao courageously accepted the challenge. They uprooted themselves from their tribe and ventured into unfamiliar territory.

They found themselves in a new environment, assuming leadership over a fragmented and contentious congregation. Through the wisdom bestowed by God and their commitment to fervent prayer and personal growth, however, the church experienced a revival. It transformed into a place of prayer and worship, becoming a beacon of light for the entire region.

After a couple of years, the church's leadership discovered a tribal group residing in the nearby mountains. Upon visiting this resistant and distant tribe, Ansulao and his team witnessed a remarkable softening of the elders' hearts. In due course, the church became a source of blessing and a missions force for this previously unreached tribe.

THE MIRACLE OF MULTIPLICATION

Numerous other accounts abound where the Holy Spirit prompted us to relinquish control and entrust the work to indigenous people.

What did this mean for us? Did we retire and sit back in restful days? Absolutely not! The decision to entrust the work to indigenous leaders opened up countless opportunities for us. In truth, it placed us exactly where we needed to be—as a support system for them. Just as the apostle Paul supported Timothy, Titus, and others, we now functioned as a support system for many indigenous pastors, leaders, and missionaries.

Our support manifests through establishing and nurturing relationships. We walk alongside them through their struggles, victories, and challenges. We also provide financial support by offering salaries until they reach a point of self-sustainability. This is where we allocate our funds—empowering them. Through the assistance of kingdom-minded financial partners, we have created a financial foundation to bolster the indigenous people's efforts in reaching the unreached tribes surrounding them.

Additionally, this new paradigm has given us the opportunity to share these testimonies with churches across the United States and the world. We aim to continue being a voice for indigenous mission leaders, inspiring people to respond to God's call and encouraging the indigenous population to take up the mantle and run with it.

Speaking of taking up the mantle and running with it, remember how I said just a little while ago that it really is God's plan to raise up workers for His harvest? The whole point of this book, and what makes it worth writing at all, is that it helps to raise you up and send you out into God's harvest.

All these stories are wonderful, and I'm grateful that I've been blessed to live them, but they all happened because of the divine power of the Holy Spirit. If you've read all the way from the beginning of this book, you know I'm just a country boy from a small town. I said yes, and I have kept saying yes ever since. I've made plenty of mistakes too, but I've kept saying yes despite the continual challenges of life.

Is anything hindering you from doing the same? Do you think you don't know how to hear God's voice? I didn't either, and sometimes I'm still unsure, but God is faithful to help us. Do you believe finances will be a problem? Well, as I've told you, commit your work to the Lord, work diligently, and I promise you that this will never be a problem. Do you not know where to go? I didn't either until I started using what was given to me. I started with my local youth group worship team. Where can you start serving God? Start there and let Him guide you from there to wherever He wants you to be.

So much of what I have seen the Father do among the indigenous peoples of the Pacific Islands would never have happened if I kept trying to do it all myself. It makes perfect sense yet somehow still feels novel to say that God's kingdom grew more when more people labored at it than when I worked alone. I encourage you to learn from that. Don't just read this book and celebrate that God is working through my life. Join me in serving God and let's celebrate together what He does through both of us!

The work of the Lord always starts from within. It's an inner work that will eventually reveal the fruit in a matter of time. The inner work can only be established through connecting and staying connected to the source of life—Jesus who was, is, and will eternally be the Son of God. No work can be good unless it's directly connected to Him. All work is meaningless unless it comes from the heart. Embrace the refinement. Undertake the inner working of the Holy Spirit with a happy attitude and, trust me, your life and work will be good.

For me, ministering and establishing God's kingdom in Southeast Asia and the Pacific Islands has truly been an adventure filled with challenges, breakthroughs, and lessons learned. As we continue this incredible journey, we remain committed to following the Holy Spirit's leading, empowering indigenous leaders, and seeing the gospel spread far and wide. Our hearts are filled with gratitude for the unwavering support of our partners and the prayers of believers worldwide. Together we press on, united in the vision of seeing every tribe, tongue, and nation worshiping at the feet of Jesus.

SIXTEEN
BE EVERGREEN

Gladys and I knew in our hearts that we were dedicated to reaching the unreached people in Southeast Asia and beyond. We knew we should change our mindset from thinking primarily about short-term missions to planning and investing in long-term missions. We knew that we should properly put down roots, not just for our family but for our missions work.

A farmer who plants seasonal crops, like tomatoes, will expect its produce to come in two to three months. Once the harvest comes, the farmer reaps its produce, and then cuts the plant down and starts over again the next year. When a farmer plants fruit trees, however, his method requires a different approach. He will have to cultivate and protect the young seedling trees from the elements and from animals that will eat the leaves. He must do this for five to eight years before fruit will even begin to form. Small saplings do not have the deep roots or large canopies that give trees the extra nutrients and energy that allow them to bear fruit, so trees spend all they have just to put down deep roots and stretch out large canopies. The roots need to go down deep to receive nutrients and the canopy branches need to stretch out to receive as much sunlight as possible. After years under the farmer's care, the tree will be strong and bear much fruit. The farmer is pleased and can step back to watch the tree produce fruit year after year with less work than at first.

In my own heart, I knew the Lord made it clear that our work in the nations would be like a fruit-bearing tree instead of a seasonal crop. Not having any money, a proper team, or a strategic plan on how to start an international ministry, I was totally dependent on the Holy Spirit. I wasn't necessarily trying to start an international missions organization, but I wanted something real and organic that would produce God's abundant harvest under the protocol of God and not man.

One early winter morning as I sat in a rocking chair in my living room, watching the sun rise slowly above the horizon, I could see some evergreen trees that outlined the border of my property. Because it was in the middle of the winter when the leaves are gone from the trees, the evergreen trees stood out, being just as green and abundant as they are in the summer. Instantly, a prayer rose inside me, saying, "Lord, whatever you do through us, let it be evergreen."

When I prayed that prayer, it resonated in me like a well-tuned guitar. It resonated so well, in fact, that I started praying that prayer over and over again. Each morning and every moment that I could, those words rolled off my lips. What I wanted was God's work to be evergreen, bearing fruit for years to come, even after I pass and move into eternity. Psalm 92 says beautifully what was on my heart:

> The righteous flourish like the palm tree and grow like a cedar in Lebanon. They are planted in the house of the Lord; they flourish in the courts of our God. They still bear fruit in old age; they are ever full of sap and green, to declare that the

Lord is upright; he is my rock, and there is no unrighteousness in him. (Psalm 92:12–15)

This was it! The Lord gave me a strong desire to be deeply rooted in Him. I wanted to be so deeply rooted in Him, receiving the fullness of His kingdom, that the fruit would produce naturally. I didn't want to have to strive to produce fruit; I wanted it to come naturally and organically.

The Lord knows that without Him, I am not righteous. I couldn't ever obtain Him by working or doing things better. It was never about working or doing better, but it was always about abiding and being rooted in Him. My prayer was to become evergreen. Ultimately, I was seeking His righteousness and kingdom. I didn't want my work to be halfhearted; I wanted to live a life wholeheartedly for Him.

I didn't intend to build an international ministry; I simply intended to seek Jesus's kingdom and righteousness. The Lord, the master farmer, planted a seed in me that wasn't a seasonal crop, it was a fruit-bearing tree. I knew that in order to make a fruit tree survive the first few years of development, it needed attention, protection, and intentionality. We felt that for us, this meant building a team. Our team was a group of widely experienced people who had the same heart and passion to reach the unreached with God's redeeming love.

A COMMUNITY FOR REACHING NATIONS

That's how Evergreen Missions was formed. It is technically an international missions organization now, but our heart is for it to be a community because it started as we came together regularly to worship, pray, and strategize with long-term goals on how to reach the nations. The Lord continued to do a deep work in us as we submitted our work to Him. Below is some basic language we created for what was in our heart as a community:

Evergreen Missions is an international missions movement working to reach the unreached and touch the untouchable with God's redeeming love. Our desire is to help empower indigenous people in carrying out the Gospel of Jesus Christ from generation to generation. We believe that indigenous people have all it takes to be flourishing evergreen trees, planted in the house and courts of the Lord. We believe there is a grace on Evergreen Missions to sow the seeds of God's Kingdom among unreached peoples and maintain those fields until there is a great harvest of God's fruit among the nations.

We love God and we love people. We desire that all of the ministry that comes from us would be evergreen—fruitful and from the heart of God.

With all of the essential pieces in place—built in connection with our God and in community with each other—we returned to Asia and the Pacific with intentionality to empower the locals to reach their own people. It certainly took many years to develop because, as I mentioned before, ministry rests on the foundation of relationships, not on organizations or formulas. Returning to the nations and empowering the locals would take years and years of discipleship, focus, risk, and dependence on the Lord. But with much grace from God, the fruit has been tremendous.

Over the course of several years, we spent our energy, time, and focus on empowering the indigenous people to reach their own people. Many individuals, churches, and organizations began partnering with us in the vision God gave us. We created a giving platform that gives people the opportunity to sow into the ongoing work of the gospel in the nations. People can give one-time or recurring monthly donations. We emphasize the importance of accounting for every penny that comes into our hands, knowing the moneys are God's resources for the gospel to reach the nations. We created a financial team to steward this with multiple levels of accountability.

With the framework the Lord gave us, we continued to share the gospel diligently, train and equip leaders, and empower locals to spread the gospel to unreached people groups. We continued our missions work in most of the areas that I have written about in this book, but the ministry of the Lord has continued to grow and spread so that it has now reached many nations. I don't want to go into much detail on this because I want this book to mostly focus on the beginning days of our ministry, because that is where we learned to hear and respond to the leading of the Lord.

CONCLUSION COMMISSION

In all the stories you have just read, I pray one thing above all has been clear to you. I have certainly not written all these testimonies so you can be impressed by my exploits or the exploits of those I've worked with in these stories. Far from it! I'm not here to toot my own horn; I'm here to encourage you in saying, "You can hear His voice too!"

If I could, I know you can! In fact, God deeply desires to speak to us and for His children to hear, know, and follow His voice. As Jesus said, "My sheep hear my voice, and I know them, and they follow me" (John 10:27).

More than anything else, that is what I hope and pray you take with you from this book. I want you to know that you can experience the same kind of powerful testimonies in your life. You just need to believe what God says to you and say yes to Him. Don't just say you are willing, but also obey Him when He says to do something. As you've seen in my stories, His instructions won't always make sense, but He will still make a way for you as you move forward in obedience.

I'm positive that your testimonies aren't going to look like mine. They will be unique to whatever God is leading you into. Not all people are called to minister to unreached people groups. What's more, hearing God's voice is not always about doing things for Him. Sometimes His voice will lead you into a season to be still and know that He is God.

God speaks in so many different ways. In whatever ways He speaks to you, I pray that this book motivates you to seek His voice by abiding in Him.

My prayer is that this book has inspired you to lean into Him. There are many other things I'd like to share, but perhaps that's for another book down the road. For now, I'd like to leave you with a blessing I have written. This blessing comes from my heart as a fellow brother in Christ. Please receive it as you open your heart for what the Father has for you in your next season.

THE EVERGREEN BLESSING

I bless you to hear and know the Shepherd's voice. May you walk in tune with the rhythms of heaven and earth as they dance. May your cup be filled with the joy and laughter of God's pleasure over you. May the obedience of your walk be the core of your soul. With your hands open and feet planted, eyes forward and ears tuned in, you will respond to the ever-present voice of the Creator. Be filled with His Spirit and let the light of His Son be your guide. Be evergreen. Be fruitful even to old age. Though you may only sow the seed or water the ground, I bless the faith within you to know God's harvest will grow.

PARTNERING WITH EVERGREEN MISSIONS

Walking in obedience to God's voice in your own life is the best way to partner with Evergreen Missions. I know from my experience of speaking in churches, however, that you might feel stirred to partner with us in other ways as well, including supporting us financially or joining our prayer team. If you do, while I didn't write this book as a sales pitch or support letter, I do rejoice in any kind of partnership for the sake of the gospel. Finances and prayer are indispensable supports to us in our work among indigenous peoples.

If you want to support us, continue following us, or simply learn more about us, you can find Evergreen Missions online at evergreenmissions.com. You can donate to us directly from there by clicking the "Partner" tab. You'll find options on that page for either one-time or recurring gifts, and you can sign up to receive our newsletter there as well to follow us more closely. Our main base is in Moravian Falls, North Carolina, where we have a missions farm that helps train and launch missionaries. We also steward a prayer and worship community in Moravian Falls.

EVERGREEN INSTRUMENTS

In the same year that we formed Evergreen Missions, we also formed a business called Evergreen Instruments. We formed a team of craftsmen who hand-make musical instruments from various countries around the world. The purpose of Evergreen Instruments is to see the redemption of extinct or nearly extinct musical instruments and to help preserve them for the generations to come. We also believe ancient instruments are an invitation to innovate, reimagining their designs to accommodate our modern musical scales and patterns. We have built over five hundred indigenous musical instruments at the time this book is written.

Musicians of all levels from all over the world purchase our instruments. This has inspired people to learn other instruments besides the typical guitar, drum set, piano, or other common instruments. It has especially encouraged indigenous people to play their own indigenous instruments. It is deeply gratifying when we see this happen because we ultimately desire that the instruments will be used to glorify and worship God by releasing the sounds of the nations to Him. We continually seek to make high-quality, long-lasting instruments that glorify God.

Evergreen Instruments is currently online at evergreeninstruments.com, and we currently have two shops—one in Moravian Falls, North Carolina, and another in the Philippines.

ABOUT THE AUTHOR

Caleb and Gladys Byerly love Jesus. Based in Moravian Falls, North Carolina, they intentionally raise their five kids and steward the work of the Lord in their region. Caleb and Gladys run Evergreen Missions, a team that focuses on reaching the unreached people groups in Southeast Asia and the Pacific Islands. Their mission is obtained by the flow of responding to God's voice, maintaining kingdom relationships, and unlocking creative ideas from God.

Caleb runs Evergreen Instruments, an instrument-making company focused on redeeming, innovating, and preserving ancient instruments from around the world. Their focus is to expand the kingdom of God and set strong biblical-based foundations for communities to grow for generations to come.

Made in the USA
Columbia, SC
04 December 2024